JEWISHNESS
AND THE
HUMAN DIMENSION

JEWISHNESS
AND THE
HUMAN DIMENSION

Jonathan Boyarin

Fordham University Press NEW YORK 2008

Fordham University Press has no responsibility for the persistence or accuracy of URLs for external or third-party internet websites referred to in this publication and does not guarantee that any content on such websites is, or will remain, accurate or appropriate.

Library of Congress Cataloging-in-Publication Data

Boyarin, Jonathan.
    Jewishness and the human dimension / Jonathan Boyarin.
        p. cm.
    Includes bibliographical references.
    ISBN 978-0-8232-2922-2 (cloth : alk. paper) –ISBN 978-0-8232-2923-9 (pbk. : alk. paper)
        1. Judaism and science.   2. Judaism and the social sciences.3. Jews—Historiography.   4. Human ecology—Religious aspects—Judaism.
5. Judaism and culture.   6. Jews—Identity.   7. Globalization.
8. Difference (Philosophy)   I. Title.
    BM538.S3B67   2008
    296.3'7—dc22

                                                                    2008034826

Printed in the United States of America
10 09 08   5 4 3 2 1
First edition

CONTENTS

Therefore, man was created singly. . . . [T]o teach the greatness of the Holy One, Blessed is He: For a man mints many coins from one mold, all similar to one another; but God minted all humans from the mold of Adam, and not one of them is like his fellow.

Mishnah Sanhedrin 4:3

Naturally, one must wish for the planet that one day it will experience a civilization that has abandoned blood and horror. . . . But it is terribly doubtful whether we can bring such a present to its hundred- or four-hundred-millionth birthday party. And if we don't, the planet will finally punish us, its unthoughtful well-wishers, by presenting us with the Last Judgment.

Walter Benjamin

No planet, no Jews.

Elissa Sampson

*Introduction: The Human Dimension
and the Life / Study System*

What are the two terms in the title of this book? "Jewishness," though perhaps unfamiliar, presents no problems; roughly, I mean by it all associations that gather around the substantive "Jew" or "Jews" and around the modifier "Jewish." But what do I mean by linking that to something as potentially grandiose or mystifying as "the human dimension?" First of all, I mean to indicate a view of Jewishness as first and foremost one of the strategies (or sets of strategies) for sustaining the life of *Homo sapiens*, that is, for integrating creaturely mortality with symbolic consciousness.

"Mortality," here, implies in turn the temporal and spatial bounds, and the limited integrity of the organism. Decades ago John Dewey articulated these dimensions as frames for human being and experience: "Space . . . becomes a comprehensive and enclosed scene within which are ordered the multiplicity of doings and undergoings in which man engages. Time . . . is the organized and organizing medium of the rhythmic ebb and flow of expectant impulse, forward and retracted movement, resistance and suspense, with fulfillment and consummation."[1] But the human organism experiences these dimensions as a unified timespace, for, as I have written elsewhere, when we stop in time we dissolve in space.

Humans are animals; Jews are animals, shocking as it is (still!) to write or say it; and our dimensionality—our delimitation in time and space—provides us with both the moral problems we have to address and the resources for that address. Our discourses of identity, of "who we are," are tied inescapably to the borderline that is our skin, but through our symbolic consciousness we constantly reach beyond and within that boundary.

It might seem gratuitous to insist on the seemingly obvious facts that what is Jewish is encompassed within what is human; that what is human is inescapably conditioned by our creatureliness; and that the very possibility of Jewish as of human life is, if not fully within our own power, certainly very much a matter of our own responsibility—were we not so accustomed still to thinking of the symbolic or cultural realms of human life as somehow divorced from, and generally as somehow qualitatively superior to, these material conditions of our discourse. That habit of divorcing and separation creates something I am inspired, by Gail Rubin's identification of "the sex / gender system,"[2] to call in turn the life / study system. Rubin's essay pointed to a naturalized identification of sex and gender—the assumption that "male" and "female" are perfect binaries and equally valid in biology and culture. It made its critical point by insisting that biology is *not* destiny; it showed that ideological categorizations of humans do not map perfectly onto biological categories.

My critique starts rather from a naturalized separation of intellectual work, of scholarship and study, from what is glibly called "real" or "ordinary" life. Although I do not purport to dismantle that distinction entirely, I do insist that it is both functional and highly contingent, and I do want to help desolidify it, largely by showing in these essays how my scholarly inquiries grow out of the times and situations in which I write them. Too much criticism, especially when generated within academia, appears oracular, inapproachable, incomprehensible, or irrelevant to most of those whom such criticism desperately seeks to touch, partly because it fails to reveal its own contingency. And what a loss! For the text is never given beforehand; it is always discovered, it is always new. It is never quite what the author intended, for no human "author" can divine how his or her intentions will intersect with the conditions of their enactment. If authorship is not quite dead, we do well no longer to treat it as the external effect of solitary genius or stubborn mediocrity. As Hannah Arendt writes, in a book whose title may in truth be the most direct inspiration for this one's, "It is because of this already existing web of human relationships, with its innumerable, conflicting wills and intentions, that action almost never achieves its purpose; but it is also because of the medium, in which action alone is real, that it 'produces' stories with or without intention as naturally as fabrication produces tangible things."[3]

The idea of the solitary hero whose intentions are carried out despite the world's impingement is linked to the idea of an autonomous culture that sustains its essential patterns notwithstanding the impingements of otherness and of the temporal contingency we call in retrospect "history." I mean culture in two primary senses here: first, as in the designation of "a culture," one of the putative sets of encompassing symbolic frameworks to which every human being is sometimes still supposed to belong; and second, as a distinctive aspect of human existence per se.[4] If I insist on leaving some rhetorical space for the integrity of cultures in the first sense (here, most pertinently, for Jewishness in its varieties), it is only because refusal to do so would imply that the academic study of Jewishness is somehow not only outside of but also perspectivally superior to Jewishness itself; and that I do not believe. If I insist likewise on leaving some rhetorical space for the autonomy of the symbolic character of human existence per se, it is primarily because our discourse about "culture" takes place within it and is impossible without it; this is a significant condition and results in an "appearance" of autonomy that is more than merely illusory.

In any case, the rhetorical distinction between Jewish study and Jewish life, as between the life and the study of Jewishness, is one of the key ways in which Jewishness is both constructed and delineated. The famous Jewish emphasis on study is neither unambiguous nor, certainly, an unmitigated good. The Israelites' response to the giving of the Commandments—*na'ase venishma*, we will do and we will listen—is commonly taken not only to indicate a foundational faithful obedience, but also to mark a priority of praxis in Judaism, sometimes understood as being in contrast to other proximate systems of rhetoric and agency. Talmudic literature famously encompasses two genres—*aggada*, or interpretive narrative, and *halakha*, or normative legal dispute—that can be taken as respectively embodying understanding and action, but the two are also known, by the tradition itself, to be intermingled rather than mutually exclusive. An emphasis on the primary valuation of contemplation, tradition, and discourse leads to unambiguous assertions by the Talmud's rabbis of their own superiority and indeed their special rights (such as freedom from taxation). Money, in premodern diaspora communities and in many Jewish worlds today, serves as a means to "buy Torah" in the form of a diligent son-in-law or of time to study. Most consequentially throughout, the general restriction to males of access to Jewish study was justified by and powerfully sustained the implicit assumptions that males were the primary and proper agents of Jewishness in general.

Revolt against a perceived obsession with the separate world of study is part and parcel of the "modernization" of Jewishness in the last two centuries or more. This obsession is cast as elite, recherché, mandarin, oppressive, and conducive to neurasthenia and ineffectual melancholia. Even within the academy, the rubric of "Jewish studies" becomes less exclusively focused on a tradition of textual criticism and opens more broadly to what at least one major university's research center calls "the study of Jewish life." Surely this move invites new ways of thinking about the Jewish as human, quite different from an earlier effort to show the Jewish roots of "universal" ideals. Its promise may be vitiated, however, to the extent that it may seek to realign the criteria of academic scholarship in accordance with presumed normative "Jewish community" values and opinions. Such slippage implies a reduction of the critical autonomy that, in large measure, justifies the existence of the university as an institution.

For this reason, as well, I do not propose to jettison the life / study system in Jewishness or elsewhere. Still, "the career and destiny of a living being are bound up with its interchanges with its environment, not externally but in the most intimate way,"[5] and that is of course true of the living being whose name appears under the title of this book. These essays grow out of the idiosyncratic intersections of my life and study, and to a great extent, each one tells the story of its own genesis. Some may seem more celebratory of ethnicity or of the past, others to harshly criticize the impulse toward nostalgia at a time of crisis when the horizon of the species seems drastically limited in the dimension of the future. A palpable desire for communion with the dead, rationalizable as the effort to retain and transmit resources for the future, is challenged and sometimes overwhelmed by the conviction that there may be no future if the crisis of the present is not attended to first.

I have little to add at this juncture by way of a general prescription for balancing these contrasting demands other than to say, once again, that our human potential is limited to the extent that we indulge long either in the comforting chauvinisms of a collective name or, alternatively, in the presumption that it is possible to live as a "generic" human being. Accordingly, investigating the link between Jewishness and the human dimension means, among other things, that sometimes "Jewish studies" will explicitly concentrate on names other than "Jew." This is not to deny that within the idioms of Jewishness, there are lessons for the possibility of meeting—adequately if not "successfully"—the challenge of sufficiently reorganizing the species so as to survive for the foreseeable future. But the emphasis here is, at least as much (and as the second epigraph suggests), on the specieswide challenge as it impinges on the possibility of speaking as a Jew, or to speak of Jewishness, today and tomorrow.

A word here about the context of those chapters that do not contain accounts of their own origins. Nearly all of these writings began as oral talks, and I have deliberately left the marks of those original occasions. By contrast, I wrote Chapter 2, "Responsive Thinking," for a volume arising out of a conference I had not in fact attended: its context, therefore, is Wesleyan University in Connecticut, where I was teaching when the request for this essay came.[6] Chapter 3 was written and delivered as the inaugural lecture of the Rutgers Interdisciplinary Humanities Center's Undergraduate Speakers Series in February 2004. Chapter 4 was written for a conference at the University of Wisconsin in April 2004 titled "Out of Europe: Time, Place and Memory Since 1945"; as is true of Chapter 7, much of it is inspired by the conference title. Chapter 5, which dates from October 2005, was my inaugural lecture as the Beren Professor of Modern Jewish Studies at the University of Kansas, a place I miss dearly now that it, too, is no longer even a part-time home. Chapter 6[7] does begin by explaining its genesis, though not that I met Meir Katz when he was a summer associate at the same fine firm where I was then still doing my best struggling to make a legal career for myself. Chapter 7 was first delivered at a conference called Sex and Religion in Migration at Yale University in September 2005.

Lest anyone be disappointed, let me add only that these pages are inevitably inadequate and do not purport to constitute a new system or synthesis. It cannot be otherwise, since they catch me at the limits of my knowledge and thinking. May God grant that we be privileged to continue the conversation.

I

A Jewish Introduction to the Human Sciences

Some years ago—at a time when I was not yet a professor and did not know whether I ever would become one—I was nevertheless invited to participate as an outside consultant in the end-of-year deliberations of the Jewish studies committee at a certain fine liberal-arts college in the Northeast. Along with the other visitors, I was asked, among other things, to spend one session sharing and discussing with the committee a sample Jewish studies course syllabus of mine. Just before the session, I sat down and drafted an outline for a course with the same title as tonight's lecture. That *this* was the syllabus I invented was inspired, I think, by my having listened to the "inside" faculty and become aware of a sharp and perhaps even bitter divide in their ranks. Some held that there was something distinctively "Jewish" about Jewish studies (and hence, that Jewish studies properly should have its own academic structure, a question perhaps entangled with whether it is particularly "for Jews"). Others, to the contrary, argued that the proper and rigorous academic study of Jews could be carried out only within the framework of established disciplines and their ordered methods and standards.

The debate appeared to me to turn on whether the designations "Jew" and "Jewish" were to be taken as *given*—hence ready and adequate containers for explorations of their meanings; or as *constructed*—hence somehow not quite reliable and in need of critical regard from some other, more solid standpoint. Characterizing the debate this way was convenient for me, since much of my stock in trade for the past decade and more has been to show the interplay of "given" and "constructed" aspects of human identities. It struck me, therefore, that I could contribute to the committee's deliberations by outlining a course syllabus emphasizing the necessarily linguistic or symbolic character of all human existence—and thus of names such as "Jew" along with reflexive debates about the status of such names. But if that were all, I would be proposing only an introductory course in cultural anthropology. The course needed to show as well that when we start by undertaking the critical examination of the name "Jew" (what we might call its history), we quickly raise questions about human existence and its linguistic character. I was proposing, though I did not quite phrase it this way then, that the most vigorous, the broadest, and yet the most focused introduction to the study of Jews and Jewishness is within an evolutionary perspective on *Homo sapiens* as the symbol-making, language-using animal, while the symbolic character of Jewishness, and the role of the name "Jew" in the history of Western semiotics, makes Jews good to think about human nature with. An underlying thesis of this syllabus, I now realize, is one that I accept almost as a truism but others do not, and that is the inevitability, for humans, of intermediate and powerful, but not fully autonomous, spheres of identification between the level of the individual and that of the species as a whole. To be critically responsible—to have the course rejoin the human, the humanities, the social sciences—the course would also have to show, through the example of Jews and Jewishness, that such intermediate levels are not necessarily, perhaps almost never, "whole cultures," that the fit between collective name and various being is always an imperfect one.

To my relief and somewhat to my surprise, I apparently managed to communicate something of this big idea. Maybe I communicated more than I intended, since one faculty member's response was, "Well, in that case I suppose we can just hire Jonathan to do all of our Jewish studies." They didn't; neither did I quite dare inquire further what he meant by that, though I couldn't help taking it as a criticism of my overweening pretense.

In any case, I have not yet had the opportunity to test my syllabus in the laboratory of a seminar. Unwilling to abandon it or to wait indefinitely for the opportunity to do so, I will attempt here to talk it through.

I begin with some apprehension of the risks of undertaking what might be called a "Jewish anthropology." As a graduate student decades ago, I once appeared on a Yiddish talk show on Paris radio. When I explained that I was a student of *yidishe antropologye*, an elderly fellow guest was perplexed: "But that's what the Nazis did!" I suppose I said *antropologye* then in order to avoid having to explain what *etnografye* meant, but my choice of words was a bad one, since it implied to her (as it certainly did for Nazi scientists) a Jewishness that was a difference in nature.

Yet here I go again, speaking of collective identities in ways that may imply a firm distinction between nature and culture. I trust that any risk I run by speaking of a "Jewish introduction" is a different one from that of being thought racist; rather, it is the kind that goes currently by names such as *essentialism, triumphalism,* and *chauvinism.*

Just a few weeks ago, when I presented some new material about my synagogue on New York's Lower East Side to a university anthropology department, I was faced with a challenge of this kind: "How do you deal with the problem of studying your own group?" The question was neither a friendly nor a sympathetic one, and in response I provided not so much an answer as various rejoinders: I pointed out that when I began graduate school, it was considered morally important to avoid cultural imperialism, and thus the study of what we conventionally call "one's own" group seemed a neat solution; I admitted that I was in any case motivated to go to graduate school not so much by abstract intellectual curiosity as by a focused nostalgia for the Yiddish-speaking world; and I pointed out as well, mostly in jest, that, insofar as I am a student of Polish Jews, I do *not* study my own people: my ancestors were, rather, Litvaks, that is, Lithuanian Jews.

In fact I was unprepared for the question, since seeing the study of "one's own" group as problematic is nearly unique to cultural anthropology, and nearly passé even there—though it might well be worth exporting to other fields, such as the academic study of "Judaism" as a religion, where the Jewishness of most practitioners is taken for granted.

I could have done better, which is to say, by the time I got on the plane the next morning I had what I thought was a better way of addressing my questioner's challenge: Insofar as the "problem" of writing about one's own group might reside in an impulse to sentimentalize its continued collective existence—to minimize its repressions and exploitations, internal and external—I would try to remember that anthropology, being a philosophical humanism, has no theoretical tolerance for chauvinism, for what Derrida refers to as "discrimination" rather than "discernment."[1] Is there not a risk that critical studies of one's own group, understood as "demystification," will discriminate rather than discern, much as there is a risk, more obvious to us, that studies of the other will portray her as stuck in some developmental place outside or "behind" us? Moreover, any attempt to police a research practice grounded in firmly existing, and firmly contrasting, collective identities between the researcher and her subjects will founder on the close examination of those identities. As many thinkers, of whom Judith Butler comes to mind most readily, have pointed out in recent decades, that I am not "that name"[2] does not mean there is a place outside naming, outside all contamination of perspective by collective names, from which I could speak.

On the same recent visit, I was provoked to speak of the evolutionary perspective in anthropology, and I propose that this evolutionary perspective is a way out of the seeming dilemma between knowing that there is no Archimedean point for analysis of identity and knowing at the same time that it is illusory to rest firmly at some place taken as solid ground. Though I can only nod to it here, there is a *philosophical* import to the assertion of evolutionism combined with the *refusal* of racism. Again, Derrida: "Racism always betrays the perversion of man [the human], the 'talking animal.' It institutes, declares, writes, inscribes, prescribes. A system of marks, it outlines space in order to assign forced residence or to close off borders. It does not discern, it discriminates."[3]

I take this as a curiously "humanist" statement for Derrida, occasioned perhaps by the occasion of addressing South African apartheid. What does he mean by "perversion," and what work does the apparent privileging of speech do here? Why does he assert, contrary to the thesis of his *Grammatology*, that what is human is properly a speaker, and that racism, as a "perversion" of that nature, that identity, is what "writes"? Taken by itself, this aperçu reflects an older association of orality with primitive immediacy, and of writing with civilized alienation and domination. In any case (by which I mean to indicate something important that is left aside for now), the notion of discernment seems to suggest here a more fragile intelligence than does that of discrimination. When what is being discerned is human, it implies a continuity or contingency of community with the other human that it discerns.

And with that, let me return to the conceit that the occasion of this consideration is indeed a *syllabus*. I note at the outset that my selection of texts may seem haphazard and no doubt is. There is plenty of wisdom out there, adequate for our collective survival, constituting or articulating a kind of nuanced "realism" that the scholars of metaphoric reason George Lakoff and Mark Johnson describe as "about being in touch with the world in ways that allow us to survive, to flourish, and to achieve our ends" (*halavay!*). This wisdom is of course not "ultimate," never "the last word."[4] The messages have been sent, are embodied in books and other media; what is most pressing is their dissemination.

Now let me begin to speculate, hypothetically, on what shape such a course might actually take. I start with three questions.

First question: How long and how often would such a course be conducted or, better, enacted? What would it mean to declare a *term* to such an investigation—to devote a quarter, a semester, or even a year to "Jewishness and the human dimension," rather than all the time we have before us and behind us? What would it mean to teach it once, as opposed to more than once? If repeated enough, would it take on something of the aspect of an autumn ritual? What if, to be utterly grandiose for a moment, it became a kind of worldwide *daf yomi*, a curriculum studied simultaneously in various places around the world like a daily page of the Talmud? What kind of "imagined community" might that create?

Second question: Would or should there be any kind of prerequisites, or in less bureaucratic terms, what kinds of already acquired literacy, if any, should be required for participation? To paraphrase Spivak's "Can the Subaltern Speak?" (as so many have before me), "can the student"—can any student—speak? I am tempted to state a preference for students who have taken at least one other Jewish studies course *or* a cultural theory course (anthropology, psychology, literary theory—not as "foundation," but in order to be able to contribute to the seminar more effectively).[5] Yet I note that this *or* creates some kind of presumption of structural equivalence between Jewish studies and "cultural theory," somewhat (but to a real and dangerous extent) as if one were to say that a prerequisite for the course is that one already *be* either

Jewish or human. By setting out prerequisites, we would in any case be reproducing categories of disqualified witnesses, analogous to those the Babylonian Talmud lists (in Sanhedrin 24b): along with the well-known women, incompetents, and minors, dice players because their occupation does not "benefit the general welfare." At any rate, to exclude those who are not sufficiently verbal—in Jewish or in human idioms—is dangerous and presumptuous if it is "the Jewish" and "the human" that are the objects we are setting out to discover or paths we are trying to discern; hence, perhaps it is best not to state any prerequisites other than *desire for dialogue* (but how would we determine even that, and really how can we know in advance that we will be in a position to indulge in *any* principle or practice of exclusion?)

To ask such questions about gatekeeping at the outset of the course implies as well something about evaluations at its conclusion. Objective entry requirements and exit tests suggest a model of cumulative and authoritative bodies of knowledge, rather than a model of increase in discursive competence. Testing for cumulative knowledge is effectively designed to insure, in advance, the availability of reliable criteria for the determination, administratively ironclad and unchallengeable, of success and failure, while attending to the acquisition of each participant's growing ability to intervene guarantees not simply the possibility of failure but also in a more complex (and richer!) way the inevitable falling-short of the instructor, not to mention the students.

Third question, one that I will only raise now but not try to answer: How does this syllabus, and, so to speak, the "message" of the course differ from an analogous course or courses such as: "a Native American introduction to the human sciences," or "a queer introduction to the human sciences"? Surely queers are good to think with, too—but the example of *that* collective name also makes clear that we are not dealing with so many species of the genus "culture" (at least if "cultures" are understood to be systems for structuring species continuity through the integration of symbolic and biological reproduction). In fact, I realize that designating such names of collective identities as in any way interesting or vigorous points of view for critical analysis may seem passé. I do not see them giving way any time soon to a renewed or more capacious liberal individualism. I do see, and have begun to try to articulate elsewhere, the obsolescence of any *static* use of these names, particularly in light of the threat to all discourse, and (hence) to all human being, posed by our collective degradation of the planet. Insofar as massive numbers of our fellows remain devoted to such names, to "being that name" in whatever fashion, better articulations of the story of being human with the story of those names remain vital in order for us to become, almost too late, more responsibly *human* in different ways.

This leads me to discussion of the theoretical framework I am either working within or struggling to articulate here. By "human sciences" I do not mean to restrict that framework to the *Geisteswissenschaften*, the humanities; rather, the phrase is intended to encompass (and work toward transcending the distinctions among) the "humanities," the "social sciences," cognitive science, and psychology. And even biology; but why should we have to say "even?" Why should religious studies majors not know that believers are animals? Why should they not know that taboo is not the negation of sex but its harnessing? Therefore, my perhaps idiosyncratically broad notion of the "human sciences" includes the study of "the human" as *science*, whatever the parameters of any particular human identity might be.

The course is intended to fundamentally theorize and also to try to give analytic substance to questions of:

1. *Embodiment* (though this term misleadingly suggests some existing personhood that is subsequently "placed in" a body);

2. *Situatedness* as constitutive of any sustainable reflection on human identity (as opposed, for example, to the search for an analytic stance free from "observer effects");

3. *Identity* as a product of a contingent self-organization of the living in time and space as opposed to the realization of an ideal, that is to say, essential or "ontic" category of some sort;

4. *Presentism,* a name for the tension between the recognition that our own concerns for the past are conditioned by our present situation, and the desire to allow the past to live for itself and to speak to us in its own voice;

5. *Historicism,* which (as I understand it) is sometimes taken as a complacent or sentimental tendency for sadness in view of the past, rather than concern for its effect in our world, contrasted to

6. A *politics of memory* in which past and present are fully interdependent;[6] and finally for this particular list,

7. The difference between *evolution* and *progress.* This distinction, I suggest, is vitally important for understanding the place of suffering in rhetorics of collective Jewish memory: Does knowing that evolution involves entropy and extinction as well as growth and increasing complexity not help us to understand that so much of what appears as incommensurate Jewish suffering has to do with the extraordinary range and duration of Jewish *life?*

Then doesn't it make sense to reinscribe the immense history of Jewish suffering as an extraordinary record of resistance to entropy? (Now I caution—myself first of all—that this analogy might seem, upon further examination, to be totally bogus, inasmuch as entropy in the cosmic timescale of the universe does not necessarily imply entropy in the limited scale of recorded human history; at the very least we can say that this is a provocative challenge to any remaining notions we may have of a progressive tendency toward *increased* order in human history).

Toward what kinds of curriculum do these concerns open out? One strategy is simply to pair readings that make no explicit reference to Jews but that promise to teach us something important about the human condition in general, with readings that focus on the analysis of questions in Jewishness. Consider, if you will, Stephen Hawking's *Brief History of Time* (1988) and its discussions—only partially accessible to me—of reversibility and unidirectionality in cosmic and historical time. Similar considerations, perhaps couched in even less technical physical language, inform "Timeswerve," Elliot Wolfson's astonishing introduction to his massive tome on kabbalah, *Language, Eros, Being* (2005). "Timeswerve" draws on analyses from contemporary philosophy and physics to show that time makes as much sense "going backward" as "going forward" (a point that is difficult for us to comprehend, because we are always looking "forward"). Indeed, Wolfson, a brilliant philological scholar and critic, argues for the use of twentieth-century theory to analyze thirteenth-century kabbalah not with the presentist claims that we can only analyze from our own standpoint, but rather by undermining the very claim that the past can only affect us, and not vice versa.

But not all of the key concepts in the human sciences pair as neatly with existing research on Jewishness—at least not with research that readily comes to mind. I return briefly to Lakoff and Johnson's *Philosophy in the Flesh*. An ambitious elaboration of their earlier *Metaphors We Live By*, this is an exploration of the metaphoric and linguistic constitution of reality. One might suppose that bringing home the point that the mind is not ontologically separate from the body (and let's put both or neither, but not just one, in scare quotes) brings home "Jewish" nondualism. Although such a notion is doubtless key to what initially led me to a *positive* identification with Jewishness, by now, I think, I too understand that to characterize sweepingly monism as Jewish, dualism as somehow other—Christian, say, or Greek—is to fall into dualism again. Still, remembering Jewishness in the West might caution us against easy acceptance of the assumption in Lakoff and Johnson's subtitle—again, *The Embodied Mind and Its Challenge to Western Thought*—that "Western thought" is coterminous with some idealism we might identify with Plato.

Among Lakoff and Johnson's summary points: "Reason . . . is not, in any way, a transcendent feature of the universe or of disembodied mind. Instead, it is shaped crucially by the peculiarities of our human bodies. . . . Reason is evolutionary, in that abstract reason builds on and makes use of forms of perceptual and motor inference present in 'lower' animals. . . . Reason is not 'universal' in the transcendent sense. . . . It is universal, however, in that it is a capacity shared universally by all human beings. . . . Reason is not purely literal, but largely metaphorical and imaginative."[7]

These are points pertinent to understanding aspects of the discourse of Jewishness—midrash as a form of "metaphorical and imaginative" yet serious hermeneutic reasoning, for example. Still, if you stare at some of this closely enough, it is not entirely clear what some of it means: for example, I do not know, and doubt whether Lakoff and Johnson would be able to say, what "purely literal" could possibly mean, although it may well mean something like "prior to relation"; as they say elsewhere, "We simply have no rich, purely literal understanding of mind in itself" (266). This casual denigration of the "literal," beyond reiterating an old Pauline trope, might block a readily available and complementary understanding that the word, even the *logos*, is always embodied, too.

Moreover, as I read Lakoff and Johnson's introductory presentations of various philosophical straw men—including, along with the "Kantian radically autonomous" and the "Cartesian dualistic" notions of the person, the "poststructuralist person," my objections to their characterization of this last theoretical "person" as a "completely decentered subject for whom all meaning is arbitrary, totally relative, and purely historically contingent" (5) makes me wonder whether my enthusiasm for their demolition of the former is displaced. Such enthusiastic reading is a danger of the broad, even overbroad scope I am assaying here; one risks relapse into taking certain texts, haphazardly chosen, as foundationally authoritative. (A concomitant danger is the risk of discovering these texts to be more or less unintelligible to students.)

A "key metaphor" analyzed by Lakoff and Johnson, and amply articulated in *Metaphors We Live By*, is the container metaphor, with the human body being the container par excellence. As we know from cultural studies of nationalism, the nation is commonly likened in turn to a collective body. Yet I would contend, contrary perhaps to the critical intent of some cultural theorists, that the metaphorical association between the person-body and the nation-body is not simply a question of "false consciousness," and is, in any case, not to be so readily dislodged by intellectual critique. Rather, embrace of the metaphor can be productive; it can be a tool for critique rather than merely an object of critique. Persons, like collectives, may thus be said to act in ways that preserve a certain measure of flexibility and a sufficient measure of coherence at the same time. It is no accident then that the analysis of the history of the people Israel as a constant struggle to steer between the Scylla of fossilization and the Charybdis of dissolution appears in a work titled *Entre le cristal et la fumée* (2004), between crystal and smoke, by the biologist and theorist Henri Atlan. To think about the identity of this collective as a constant reinvention of itself in between the deadly poles of crystal and smoke potentially offers—or at least I would claim, and try to convince my students that it offers—new ways of thinking about the *life-promoting* potentials of the human propensity for forming, and affirming (more or less exclusive) loyalties to, collective identifications at the subspecies level, a propensity we have no reason to assume is about to disappear, even as the development (diffusion? evolution?) of an effective species-consciousness becomes an ever more vital necessity for any conception of possible futures.

I can only list but not dwell on a few—a few more, maybe, but this time more anthropological, less literary or historical—of the basic concepts in the human sciences that this course must, or should, raise. The list includes, at minimum,

1. *Kinship*, understood not only as patterns of organizing family relations but as itself one of the "key metaphors" by which humans understand the relations between themselves and *all* others; the biblical narrative will be richly exemplary here.

2. *Mimesis* and *differentiation*, the human impulses (perhaps just one impulse) to be like and different from one's fellow. This should help the seminar to discuss the boundaries between Jews and their neighbors in terms other than "assimilation" and "ghettoization." Likewise, Freud's concept of "the narcissism of petty differences" might lead nicely into a discussion of the way Jewish identities are shaped by internal dichotomies, such as the famous ones between reified Ashkenazim and Sephardim, between Litvaks and Galitsianers (that is, Galician Jews), and more recently, between the contentious proponents of the great *latke-hamantash* debate.[8]

3. "*Race*" and "*culture*." Here it will be more than sufficient if the course conveys two fundamental points, both crucial to the ancient and modern career of Jewishness in, and as part of, the West: one is that the distinction between the two notions is vitally important, yet highly unstable, and that the twentieth-century humanist attempt to separate

them had entailed its own broad areas of blindness. The other—as brought out, for example, in Denise Buell's *Why This New Race?* (2005)—is that far from being a new, modern concept, rhetorics of identity in terms of race extend to antiquity and to supposedly "universalistic" formulations such as early Christianity.

4. The formulation of meaning through *presence* versus the formulation of meaning through *absence*. What can "meaning through absence" mean? Here is a relatively straightforward illustration: Stephen Hawking hypothetically supposes "universes that, although they might be very beautiful, would contain no one able to wonder at that beauty," but immediately follows with the insight that if they are really universes—that is, if they are truly "separate from each other" (which means, separate from our universe and the consciousness it contains)—then they cannot really "be said to exist." In those universes, God might be said to exercise "the excessive power of silence" that the Egyptian-French Jewish poet Edmond Jabès counterposes, in his *Book of Hospitality*, to the human possession of "the excessive power of speech."[9] What might students make of this? What does this speaking of absence "say" about the very format of the seminar? How is it possible to utter the word "God" in a university seminar? How is it possible to conceive a university that would avoid this word that is so human?

What "Jewish" texts, then, shall we read?

Certainly the Genesis account of the creation of the universe, which is precisely not about God's power of silence but about the structuring power of language to create a universe, and the Genesis account of the creation of humanity, which is of course not about the creation of the first Jew. Reviewing the *order* of the creation in Genesis will permit us to consider whether and how the divine, the human, and the animal share the quality of "life," and what it might mean to say that whatever Adam named things, that was their name. The myth of Babel will raise for us the necessity, and the evident desirability from a God's-eye view, of human diversity.

We will consider, most presentistically, the body in ancient Israelite religion[10] and in early Rabbinism[11] and even more so what it means to be talking about "the Jewish body" just now.

We will consider founding texts of the formulation of identity as the memory of loss: Lamentations; Nathan Nata Hannover's *The Abyss of Despair* (1983), composed to commemorate the Chmielnicki pogroms; and Sylvie-Anne Goldberg's *Crossing the Jabbok* (1996), on the Jewish culture of death and dying in early modern Prague, a text that helps to restore the link in consciousness between the living and the dead and to cast into sharper relief the sharp distinction that had been erected between them by the time and place of Sigmund Freud, who thought, accordingly, that it was psychically inappropriate to sense the dead as present.

We might read the aforementioned Edmond Jabès's foundational *Book of Questions*, a book that undoes the neat geography of Jewish "culture areas" not least by its commemoration of memorable, if fictive, East European Jewish victims, but perhaps even more profoundly because of its reiterated elaboration of an always incomplete narrative and the reiterated demand *"oui, oui, mais encore,"* "yes, but there must be more." It is to a great extent this tension between the desire for plenitude and the acknowledgment of fragmentation in representations of the (Jewish) past that makes Jewish studies an excellent laboratory in which to learn the fundamental lesson that the map is not the territory.

Reading Miriam Bodian's book about the reinvention of the

"Portuguese" Jewish community in seventeenth-century Holland,[12] we will not only articulate the notions of "invented traditions"[13] or of "imagined communities,"[14] but also more immediately recognize (the point must be made over and over) that the post-Enlightenment is not the first time a group of people has had to figure out, together, *how to be a Jewish community*.

In a "unit" (now how's that for an unexamined but profoundly structuring metaphor?) on textuality, we might consider the role of texts in the cultural politics of medieval Christian-Jewish relations.[15] Sander Gilman's *Jewish Self-Hatred: Anti-Semitism and the Hidden Language of the Jews* (1986) will raise the question of language as "container" of identity, and the further questions "contained" therein: What is a Jewish language? What is Jewish literature? What is Jewish discourse? Jeffrey Shandler's *Adventures in Yiddishland: Postvernacular Language & Culture* (2006) will introduce us to the notion of the postvernacular, that is, to the status of Yiddish today as a pointer toward collective identity more than as a medium of collective expression.

And perhaps we will have time to consider modernity as a cultural crisis in which contradictions of identity once provisionally contained in folk narrative and ritual are, as it were, stripped bare and become explosive. The text I have in mind for launching this particular point is Claudine Fabre-Vassas's *The Singular Beast: Jews, Christians and the Pig* (1997). In it, Fabre-Vassas explores how, through the medium of porciculture, pork consumption, and folklore about pigs, medieval and early modern European Christians were able to address tensions in the Christian life cycle and in the history of Christianity out of, but never fully out of, Jewishness. As those rituals were lost, modern anti-Semitism—racialist, political, exclusionary, and ultimately murderous—was being invented. We will end, then, on maybe a disturbingly conservative note, with the hint that a loss of the human capacity for even cruel ritual might sometimes be a dangerous thing.

These, in conclusion, are the goals of the course "A Jewish Introduction to the Human Sciences":

1. To provide students points of further entry into a wide range of topics in the sea of Jewishness.
2. To imbue students with a sense of the study of Jews as "good for thinking [about being human] with."
3. To foster the integration of reflection and experience.
4. To broaden and focus processes of identification (and here, as a caveat, I must express concern about how, if at all, this "goal" implies differentiation between those students or that instructor who bear the name "Jew" and those who do not).
5. To recognize that the seminar creates the instructor. And by way of plea for mercy, let my last words be a reminder that if this vision seems hasty or unfocused now, it is only because in our universe, where we remember the past but not the future, the seminar has not created its instructor, not yet.

2

Responsive Thinking: Cultural Studies
and Jewish Historiography

Although the distinction between names and things is one of the oldest in
philosophy, historians have but recently taken it into account.

—Karl Morrison

We must always be conscious . . . that we are attempting in our way to
understand their understanding.

—Karl Morrison

This is a short story about the troubled romance between the master discipline of Jewish history (perhaps more subaltern than it
has seemed from my particular perspective) and the wayward, unpredictable, "undisciplined" hybrid known as cultural studies.
Two caveats before I begin the tale. The first is that the works
(mostly quite recent) of Jewish historiography cited, held up as
models of reflexive awareness and interdisciplinary liveliness, and
once or twice taken to task here have all come to my attention in
the course of my own recent reading and research; nothing
should be inferred about any texts *not* discussed when the criteria
of inclusion are, as the statisticians say, necessarily haphazard.
Second, while I understand fully that the rubric of "cultural studies" has historically been nurtured in and around departments of
literature—and while my own thinking is very much informed by
literary theory—I find that I remain in sensibilities very much a

cultural anthropologist, and will not attempt here to draw what would in any case be implausibly definite distinctions between anthropological perspectives on the one hand, and literary-cultural perspectives on the other.[1] If forced, however, to make some more positive statement than that, I suppose I would stammer that cultural studies is the place where ethnography writ beyond the confines of the oral, the primitive, and the tribal meets literary studies (and its daughter disciplines, such as film and media studies), listening and looking beyond the canon—both together, I suppose, turning willy-nilly to face the angel of history.

My story therefore begins with the moment when, still an undergraduate but already passionate about the Yiddish culture that still lay mysteriously on the other side of my competence, I was faced with the choice of which graduate department would serve as my ticket across. At that time, fortuitously, the great American social historian Herbert G. Gutman visited the Pacific Northwest college campus where, with a small coterie of friends, I was struggling to fashion an "authentically" Jewish New York personal idiom.[2] I had the opportunity to tell Herb that I wanted to go to graduate school, learn the Yiddish language, and study modern East European Jewish life, and I asked him whether I should apply to a department of history or of anthropology. Without hesitation, he answered: "You should get a PhD in anthropology. We need historians trained in anthropology."

I followed Gutman's advice, and, perhaps because my choice was largely guided by it, I never suffered under the delusion that what I studied, in the anthropology department at the New School for Graduate Research and at the YIVO Institute for Jewish Research, was *not* history.

How could it have been otherwise, for someone who wanted more than anything else to break through the double barrier of the "shtetl myth" on one hand and the genocidal abyss of memory on the other, in order to attain something that might answer to the name "living connection" to the Jewish community world of Eastern Europe? Methodologically, I couldn't do a year of participant observation in a Jewish community such as Boiberik (at once fictional and real) in the 1930s. I had to turn to questions of memory, whether written or oral, and necessarily to the ways that the present shapes the past, and this struggle with the complexities of interpreting both written and oral "texts" led me to engagement with literary theory. More to the point (less obvious, perhaps), I couldn't fix Boiberik in the 1930s in anything like a timeless "ethnographic present"[3] or analyze the "structure" of its Jewish community in a way separate from contingency, event, external determination. When studying and writing about Polish Jewish immigrants in Paris in the early 1980s, I had to serve, *faute de mieux*, as my own consulting historian, since no professional historian had, to my knowledge, tied the ethnic and political history of interwar Poland to the ethnic and political history of Jews before and after World War II.

But I was not then, and in the professional historian's eyes have never been, a historian. And, tedious and difficult as it might be to document, it is clear that—certainly twenty-five years ago, when I was doing these graduate studies, and perhaps to a diminished extent today—there has "historically" been a hierarchy of disciplinary prestige in Jewish studies, with the historians standing very near the top, the literary critics expected to stick to literature and not to transgress the boundaries of popular culture, and the anthropologists only gradually coming in from nowhere at all.[4] An echo of this may be heard in a complaint reported from an audience member at one of the earliest conferences on the culture of Sephardic and Oriental Jewry in Jerusalem, sometime in the 1970s: "How come the Ashkenazim have history and we only have culture?"[5]

My best friends understood that my own unwillingness and inability to limit myself to the theoretical menu available within cultural anthropology, combined with the frustrating impression that only professional historians were "authorized" to speak about the past (or, saying the same thing a different way, that it is only the "history" of the past that is considered really important), and the conviction that Jewish difference had as much to teach us about general processes of domination, resistance, and identification as gender, "racial," or postcolonial difference each does, led me along with colleagues to promote the rubric of Jewish cultural studies. What I said that meant in the mid-1990s was this:

> Cultural studies is the name of a creative turbulence in a moment of crisis for the "modern West" and the liberal academy within it. It represents a struggle to provide an answer (or at any rate a response) to this crisis through discovering ways to make history, literature, and other cultural practices "work" better for the enhancement of human lives. Jews and Jewish culture both are obviously in their own state of crisis. Thus there is room for a Jewish cultural studies, one that will function in two ways: first by seeking to discover ways to make Jewish literature, culture, and history work better to enhance Jewish possibilities for living richly; and second by uncovering the contributions that Jewish culture still has to make to *tikkun olam*, the "repair of the world."[6]

I would add now that I take the rubric of cultural studies to include (beyond the relatively hortatory connotations expressed in that quotation), *inter alia* and for the purposes of this essay, an attempt to bridge the disciplinary distinctions among history, the social-scientific analysis of ritual, theology, and literature, themselves patently products of Western power / knowledge formations and the particular ways they have configured the relation between authority and identity.

I confronted these confusing questions for the first time in many years upon "returning"[7] to the academy in the fall of 2004, facing the double challenge of teaching formally for the first time in over a decade, and of teaching a course billed as "Histories of Jewish Diaspora" at that (for I, too, remain uncertainly under the spell of the historian's unique discipline and authority). Middletown, Connecticut, a place I had not known before, was thus a site of professional homecoming for me, where I knew both delight and anxiety. The delight should not be merely incidental here, as much of my concern remains, as it was when I first began graduate school nearly thirty years ago, with the specific experience of particular places ("Boiberik in the 1930s"). Thus my scribbled notes for this essay begin at an orchard a few miles east of the Connecticut River, a few miles north of Middletown, in late September, with these words:

> Pants and fingers stained with raspberries, picked at their peak purple not red (he typed "read") . . . a bit more and they're rotten. Truly ripe raspberries cannot be bought at market (William Blake asks: "What is the price of experience?") And he thinks, he articulates without voicing, a Yiddish phrase: *toem gevezn gan eden*.[8]

I had gone exploring, that late summer day, without a map, crossing eastward from Middletown over the broad Connecticut River, which flows from north to south, then driving in fact northward parallel to the river but not seeing it, thinking myself still driving east and thus, having wended my way to the Connecticut River ferry, somehow (though it was logically impossible) thinking I was still facing east.

> As I cross the river the first time, the bargeman, seeing my yarmulke, says, "Happy New Year" and the tug driver says, "It's Rosh Hashanah tonight, right?" I ask about the road north, pointing left, and he corrects me: north is to the right, gently pointing out the sun behind me to indicate the morning east. Then, pointing across the river, "That's our West Bank."

Returning a week later to the same spot, I had trouble "reorienting" myself (more properly, "reoccidenting" myself, getting through my patterned skull the notion that I was facing west). Once again, I had trouble shaking the impression that the bank I drove up on was the western one, that north was across the river to my left and south to my right. So much for the specific pleasures of place, and so much for an allegory of the difficulty of rearranging our mental maps.

It was more the anxiety that led to these reflections on the challenge of teaching a Jewish history course at Wesleyan University to bright students with a reasonable expectation that their instructor should know *what happened*, while I myself was more concerned with being able to convey a lively and "thick" description[9] of Jewish worlds that, in many cases, I was painfully aware I knew all too thinly. Moreover, I faced the same dilemma as, I suppose, any inexperienced director of a seminar in the humanities: I knew I didn't want to—couldn't, I thought—"just lecture"; and yet, without knowing the students in advance, how could I structure a discussion with the unknown?

Hence my title, a play on the stiffly formalized "responsive readings" (commonly of Psalms translated into English, or of banal modern homilies) that are central to North American Conservative and Reform Jewish prayer services (and somehow utterly different from the "call and response" patterns of African and African Diaspora public cultures). I associated responsive readings with the challenge of creating a learning dialogue with my students—who I assumed beforehand would come mostly from upper-middle-class, non-Orthodox, and quite likely suburban Jewish backgrounds. This required an odd and slightly unnerving reorientation to mainstream American styles of performing Jewishness for someone like myself who has spent the past quarter-century fashioning and fancying himself a Jew in the quite extraordinary remnants of the Jewish Lower East Side.

The phrase also represented for me the challenge of discovering my students and finding a "responsive" discussion with them.

For a seminar leader, being responsive where the script is not laid out beforehand requires both an openness to what is not known and the ability to share what my interlocutors may not have known beforehand. The work of permitting myself that openness was hampered in part by my lingering sense of trespass as a nonhistorian.

Will that sense of trespass be finally allayed or made more acute when, in the fall of 2005, I actually become a member of a history department?[10] I will, in any case, have ample further opportunities to analyze it, as attested to by this fragment from an email exchange with a future colleague over the future direction of the department:

I: What do you mean by "the value of an education in our subject"?

JC: It's a matter of degree.[11] We would doubtless all support all virtuous approaches to the subject, but not, I trust, to the point where undergraduates don't grasp the special nature of historical method, and come to view history's subject matter in a timeless presentism—always the default mode.

I did not dare to reply in a way that gave reason to suspect I had any doubts that there *was* a special nature to historical method, or that what it constituted was in any way unclear in my mind. Thus I am left to presume that my interlocutor was referring, perhaps in addition to the special kinds of documents and other evidence considered by historians in piecing together the past, to some special stance that might still be called objectivity or a concern for what actually happened (though what historian today will dare to get up and confess that she still seeks to understand history *"wie es eigentlich gewesen ist?"*). Whatever the special method was in my interlocutor's mind—and though he also made clear his awareness that at best we only ever attend to a minute fragment of what actually happened, it was the bugbear of "timeless presentism" that frightened me. The power of imagination is so important in my teaching, and, no matter how hard we must work to imagine the ways that others (distant in geographical and social time and space) are both like and different from us, I remain convinced that we can begin to imagine others only from the starting point of who we understand and imagine ourselves to be. As Esther Benbassa and Jean-Christophe Attias write: "Ask the Jews how they conceive of the other and you will soon learn how they conceive of themselves."[12] Perhaps: presentism if you will, but not "timeless presentism." Historians, too, sometimes thus insist on explicitly starting from and returning to the present; witness, for a recent example, Judith Lieu at the conclusion of her recent *Christian Identity in the Jewish and Greco-Roman World.* Having patiently traced out—drawing on all the resources of a philologist of late antiquity and on contemporary theories of the formation, maintenance, and dissolution of group identity—the existential and doctrinal dilemmas of negotiating the ways that Christians were to be kin and alien to, like and contrasted to, Jews and members of the broader Mediterranean world, she acknowledges:

> An obvious response, however, may still be that this has been *our* reading of the texts, conditioned by a twenty-first-century agenda. It may not be how anyone in the first three centuries understood what they heard, read, or wrote. The distinction between the earliest readers of the texts and ourselves as their present readers has, it might be protested, become vicariously annulled. That is, of course, always the historiographical dilemma. But in showing how early Christian texts share the same dynamics and many of the same strategies with other Jewish and Graeco-Roman texts we have sought to neutralize this objection. It does not matter that we have supplied the agenda and the framework for our reading of the texts; what matters is that by so doing we can conceive a coherent social world that encompassed and enabled differentiation among the actual lives of those whom we cannot otherwise know.[13]

This master thus contends, convincingly and with confidence, that our task is not to see others as they saw themselves but to articulate the inherited fragments of their world in a way that makes empathetic sense. It is perhaps not merely the same argument taken a step further to suggest that, beyond the need for better philology and more literacy, the ultimate payoff is the reformulation of our sense of ourselves in the present: "The more difficult and essential of the tasks is that of considering the validity of the views we hold, understanding their ideological bases, and readjusting them if they are found wanting."[14]

But here I pause, a bit stymied, almost a bit embarrassed, for two reasons: first, because this latter quote (from 1987) conveys the same vague and now somehow naïve-sounding hope or promise of liberation through criticism as does my 1996 definition of cultural studies, quoted earlier (this hope or promise is not so radical, really: it used to be called Enlightenment); second, more immediately and prosaically, because it is not clear that a meeting of undergraduates (my Wesleyan seminar) necessarily *holds* views sufficiently articulated (whether ultimately "wanting" or not) to serve as the primary basis for critical exploration of the past.

These, then, are the elements of the challenge that I faced, teaching for the first time, from the perspective of an anthropologist, a one-semester course covering the broad sweep of Jewish cultural history, trying to avoid the luxury of a Eurocentric limitation on the scope of that history, including (as happens more than we like to admit) some topics where the virtual sum total of my own information came from the assigned readings, and working with a group of students of uneven backgrounds (a couple of whom occasionally knew more than I and did not hesitate to display their knowledge).

Trying to find some kind of responsible balance in the face of this challenge, here are some techniques that I found myself repeatedly employing:

1. I found myself attending, and drawing my students' attention to, contemporary historiography (and not just primary texts) as a literary cultural artifact, getting into the habit of looking for the analytic bind an author has fallen into that is readily betrayed by the escape modifier "ironically," or watching for unsupported throwaway assertions that present themselves as being by the by, given, as having nothing do with assertions as to "history," as mere restatements of what everyone knows and agrees on.
2. I focused on, and attempted where possible to push further, the "anthropological" insights and questions raised by the material provided us by the historians.
3. I never assumed that increasing distance in time affords greater objectivity.

I will elaborate on these three points shortly, but let me make it instantly clear that I do not want to be heard as making any kind of claim, one way or the other, as to the existence of some putative *hors-texte*. On the contrary, I am trying to address the common situation of contemplating an immense sphere of human experience (for example, several centuries of Jewish life in Alexandria) through the precious but narrow and necessarily "distorted" scope of a single fifty-page essay. It makes sense, does it not, is it not properly *scientific*, to examine closely the scope and not only the view it presents? Moreover, much like anyone ambivalently welcoming and shunning the gaze of another, historians seem to invite and at the same time subtly impede this kind of interrogation. And, of course, they increasingly look to enrich their investigations with perspectives that may trespass the "special nature of historical method." Sometimes this takes place in the context of debates within their own discipline. Thus Roberto Bonfil, acknowledging Croce, writes in the introduction to his *Jewish Life in Renaissance Italy* that "all history is contemporary history, because history is an integral part of the conception of the Self and its relation to the Other."[15] Moreover, Bonfil's concern with the dialectic of collective selfhood and the collective other informs his understanding of the period about which he writes: "My purpose has been to present the history of the Jews of Italy in the Renaissance and Baroque periods from the inside. . . . [This] is the history of a coming to awareness of the Self in the act of specular reflection in the Other."[16] Isn't this the theoretical armature of interdisciplinary cultural studies?

Other historians of Jewish life appear likewise to be more ready than they once have been to acknowledge the value of perspectives from nonhistorical cultural studies. Thus Robert Chazan, in his most recent book, *Fashioning Jewish Identity in Medieval Western Christendom*, nods with his title to the influence of literary cultural studies (Greenblatt's *Renaissance Self-Fashioning*), and explicitly acknowledges "the growing influence of anthropology. Anthropological study has tended to focus on the functions that religious faiths play within societies. This has led away from the earlier judgmental posture and toward an appreciation of the diverse objectives of religious systems, with their relative successes and failures. The present study is very much a part of this newer anthropological thrust in religious studies."[17]

Curiously, Chazan cites not a single work by an anthropologist. By contrast, Judith Lieu's *Christian Identity in the Jewish and Greco-Roman World* includes a discussion titled "Boundaries," containing an extremely rich and concise summary of recent discussions (from Fredrik Barth onward) of the processual nature of ethnic identities, drawing on work by anthropologists, historians, and "literary" cultural theorists (especially Paul Gilroy).

Perhaps not too much ought to be made of the fact that Chazan incorporates the "anthropological perspective" without explicit reference to anthropologists. This should not be an occasion for the display of bruised disciplinary egos. The risk, however, is that some readers may assume that the historian has in fact already assimilated (in the form of functionalism) all that they need to know or might stand to gain from anthropology, with the result that this new perspective is explicitly acknowledged only to be ultimately held at arm's length.

Here, at any rate, are a number of examples of my points 1 (on the critical reading of history as text), 2 (on the search for the "anthropological" content sometimes partially hidden in historians' accounts), and 3 (on the difference between distance and "objectivity").[18]

Examples of Point 1

My first example is the resort to "irony" in historical narrative, which often seems to short circuit an insight nearly glimpsed by the author, and thus to present a lost but retrievable opportunity for cultural analysis. In the midst of her study of "Portuguese" Jews in seventeenth-century Amsterdam, a book that is exemplary for its sensitivity to the contingencies and pressures attendant upon the invention of Sephardic Jewishness after the departure from Iberia, Miriam Bodian writes:

> Ironically, Iberian society sometimes freely offered conversos information of which they might otherwise have been ignorant. The "Edicts of Faith," for example—proclamations calling for judaizers to come forth and confess their crimes, and for the faithful to denounce judaizers— provided detailed lists of Jewish rituals in order to inform potential denouncers what to look for. Ironically, such lists also furnished valuable information to judaizers to whom the Inquisition had systematically denied access to such knowledge.[19]

That information designed to facilitate control is often used to subvert domination is, however, a commonplace of subaltern studies. Looking closely beyond the surface "irony," therefore, enables us to do even more with Bodian's text, linking the phenomena she lucidly presents and acutely analyzes to similar processes in postcolonial situations. Similarly, when Elliot Horowitz refers to the "painfully ironic" enforcement by the Mantua Jewish community of "Jewish attendance at compulsory Christian sermons," what he is really pointing to is the fact that there is agency as well in a position of sustained subordination.[20] That phenomenon, too, is hardly unique to the Jews, but may still seem puzzling to the extent that we continue to "oscillate between what Salo W. Baron defined as *'the lachrymose conception of Jewish history'* and what, paraphrasing Baron, we might call *'the antilachrymose conception of Jewish history.'*"[21]

Another example is the use of "hydraulic" explanations for cultural change. By this I mean any explanation of cultural change that attributes the rise in one phenomenon to a decline in another, as though cultures were containers that are "naturally" filled at a certain level with *something*. Thus, for example, "The converse of this increase of secular writing in Ladino was . . . a decline in the number of publications of religious import."[22] Why and how is one a "converse" of the other? Is the vessel (the Ladino language) not affected by this change in its content (religious versus secular literature)? Why, in a move toward secularism per se, is the separate language maintained at all? Similarly, Yosef Kaplan writes that among Sephardim in Amsterdam, "Secular activity expanded into the space left vacant after the scope of Jewish law was narrowed."[23] What "space" was that? Was it still somehow "Jewish" space, and if so, why? Why did one public or communal realm give way to another, rather than leaving in its place only atomized nuclear families? I do not for a second suggest that the historians I cite here are oblivious to these questions, but that their reader's sense of the contingency of Jewish (as of any other) identity in the chronotopes they describe is blunted to the extent they fall back on rhetorics of cultural wholes when doing cultural history.

Examples of Point 2

My first example of point 2 is the turn to thick description. The phrase "thick description" refers to a renewed emphasis, in ethnography and elsewhere in cultural studies, on providing as rich a sense of the context in which cultural meanings are deployed and contended for as possible, and on holding theoretical structures in abeyance for a bit before that context is presented. In fact, the essay in which the anthropologist Clifford Geertz (regrettably, not otherwise known as an ethnographer of Jews) introduced the phrase turned on an anecdote about a Jewish Moroccan trader named Cohen.

Perhaps it was through Geertz that the trend in literary cultural studies called the New Historicism[24] acquired another stylistic pattern now shared in the writing of Jewish cultural history, to wit, my second example: the piquant opening anecdote. For an outstanding example, I will merely direct the reader to the beginning of Ray Scheindlin's article on Judeo-Arabic culture in the golden age of Islam, which offers an extended quote from the memoirs of Judah al-Harizi. The quote presents a dramatic episode about three Jewish youths who demand of a diviner that he both guess their question, "When will the Jews be redeemed from the exile, and when will the Jewish kingdom be restored?" (311), and provide the answer. But the payoff, for Scheindlin, is the evidence the story provides about social boundaries: "The story's depiction of the Jewish characters as externally indistinguishable from the Muslim masses . . . corresponds with the reality of Jewish life in the Muslim world . . . from the seventh through the thirteenth centuries" (313). Here we have a stylistic element that is fully assimilated from literary cultural studies into historiography, and to very rich effect.

Examples of Point 3

My apologies for misleading you, gentle reader: while I did exhort my students not to fall into the trap of thinking that the distant past is somehow fixed and therefore better known than our own messy present, I do not in fact find recent writings in Jewish historiography to fall into that naïve trap. Perhaps this shift toward what Judith Lieu identifies as the goal of an account that makes sense of the past, rather than an account of what really happened, is part and parcel of a greater tendency, shared now by Jewish historians, to see identity (including Jewishness) as contingent and as performed or enacted rather than as a matter of heroism and tolerance. Thus, to cite only two examples almost at random, Yosef Kaplan, at page 653 of the essay in *Cultures of the Jews* that I cited (and criticized) earlier, offers an evocative description of the pomp surrounding the conduct of services at the new Portuguese *esnoga* in Amsterdam as a conscious performance for the community itself as well as its non-Jewish neighbors. In her book on the same community, Miriam Bodian avoids falling into the trap of writing as though this community constituted itself through a simple recuperation of its true Jewishness, and leaves ever present before the reader's eyes the task of communal reinvention, and the challenge of enforcing the bounds of that new community.

Along with this understanding of identity (personal and collective) as always contingent, always in need of maintenance, reinvention, repair, thus goes a new emphasis on its boundaries, its points of contact and repulsion vis-à-vis the other, as signaled by the quote from Roberto Bonfil above and, indeed, by the preoccupations of nearly all the essays in Biale's *Cultures of the Jews*. Within the works of a single Jewish scholar, I cite Daniel Boyarin's own emphasis[25] on the shift in his thinking from a strategy emphasizing "only the positions that seemed most antithetical to 'Christian' or 'Hellenistic' ones"[26] to an emphasis on the presence "within the Talmud itself of positions much closer to those of contemporary Others in the Mediterranean world." I will cite Daniel Boyarin's most recent book, *Border Lines*,[27] to suggest that this shift in emphasis—this new tone, we might call it, in his scholarship—reflects a more general sea change, in Jewish cultural studies and elsewhere in history, anthropology, and related disciplines, from a focus on what James Scott famously called "domination and the arts of resistance" to a focus on the continuous construction, maintenance, and transgression of boundaries between ethnic and other collective identities.

Here as elsewhere the Yiddish cultural historian and sociolinguist Max Weinreich (like his son Uriel Weinreich) articulated approaches to cultural analysis decades before they became generally current: "It thus turns out that the very existence of a division [between cultural groupings] is much more important than the actual location of the division line."[28] That prescient quote aside, one early example of this new trend, perhaps early enough to be called a precursor, is Peter Sahlins's 1989 volume *Boundaries: The Making of France and Spain in the Pyrenees*. In addition to the year it was published, that book is remarkable for two other reasons: first, that it focuses on the constructed nature of what we have until recently tended to take as most natural, namely geographic boundaries between nations; and second, perhaps, that it was written by a historian who is the son of an anthropologist, Marshall Sahlins.

Certainly, the new focus on boundaries, the meetings, collaborations, and clashes that take place at boundaries to recreate and challenge them, and the methodological urgency of questioning their given nature can be detected in current scholarship on various periods and places in the history of Christianity. Thus, for example, Osvaldo Pardo, in his study *The Origins of Mexican Catholicism*, criticizes Robert Ricard's classic *The Spiritual Conquest of Mexico* as follows: "The perspective brought by Ricard rests on the notion that the Nahua and Christian religion each possessed definite and identifiable boundaries or, rather, that such demarcation is in a certain sense methodologically necessary."

Daniel Boyarin's effort to inscribe the Talmudic narrative "within a larger [ancient] Mediterranean history of sexuality" similarly recalls Ammiel Alcalay's effort, in his 1993 book *After Jews and Arabs: The Remaking of Levantine Culture*, to reinscribe Jewish literatures in several languages within a shared cultural universe of the modern-day Levant.

If I am right in detecting a trend here, we may dub it "boundary theory" or "boundary discourse." A few huge questions immediately arise on the relation of boundary theory to (1) theories of identity and difference that focus on the production of self through discourses of Othering; and (2) the theory of abjection, in which Othering by the dominant group creates or at least sustains the subaltern collective self—I will identify this as the theory put forth in Marx's "Essays on the Jewish Question," brought to us by way of Sartre. One preliminary answer to these questions may be that boundary theory permits and fosters a greater sensitivity to contiguities between collective identities, or names, without necessarily reinscribing notions either of cultural universals or of cultural diffusion.

Again, if there is some kind of shift toward a boundary discourse, toward the idea that the real action is at the margins and not at the center, what does that say about our own notions of or attachments to any collective identity now? Is our hold on some attachment to a positive projection of some sui generis core of group identity more tenuous than it was even a few short years ago? In the light of boundary theory, we might suggest, for example, that Daniel Boyarin's effort to construct Jewish difference in *Carnal Israel*—an effort close to my heart, given our intellectual kinship and our kinship tout court—as one of colonial domination and diasporic resistance is better understood as a project in boundary construction and maintenance.

If cultural studies with its emphasis on the constructed nature of all identities, personal and collective, might seem at first blush to pose a challenge to the maintenance of the Jewish and other collectives, the reverse question might be asked as well: Are there ways in which cultural studies, with its linkage both to literary scholarship and to ethnography, is *especially* congenial to approaches to Jewish cultural history? Here, for a starting point, I would point to the facility cultural studies has for seeing textuality as part of life, rather than merely the medium of a second-order representation of life. That lesson is now being absorbed, with profit, by seasoned master historians such as the medievalist Jeremy Cohen, yielding for example this shift from a frustrating attempt to sort out the "factual basis" in medieval Jewish martyrologies, to a new emphasis on the meaning of the creation and reception of the martyrologies themselves:

> While tales of martyrdom, then, perhaps can teach us something about the martyrs themselves, their ideas, and their deaths, they communicate considerably more about the *martyrologists*, those who remember the martyrs and tell their stories because they find them meaningful. Applying these principles to the extant Hebrew narratives of the 1096 persecutions, we shall see how the martyrs' stories teach us above all else about the survivors who told them.[29]

More radically perhaps, a recent essay by David Nirenberg turns the very idea of a genre of "Jewish history" back onto itself, as he examines how Jewish historiography became part of the great effort—shared, from both sides of the divide, by "Christians" and "Jews"—to determine exactly to whom those two names properly belonged, after the great confusion inaugurated by the great persecution in Spain in 1391 and the mass conversions that followed.

In this great sorting out process between 1391 and 1492, "genealogy [was elevated] to a primary form of communal memory,"[30] and the efflorescence of history writing was a key prop of that genealogical memory. "Racial" notions that—again among both Christians and Jews—became prominent at that time, by our day have, albeit imperfectly, been discarded:

> But it is fitting to end with the rise of history, because of all the products of the genealogical turn in Sepharad, it alone retains its power to convince. We now, for example, treat as so much fiction the richly illuminated *ketubbot* (marriage contracts) that Sephardic families began to produce in the fifteenth century in order to celebrate their Davidic ancestry. Yet we rarely quarrel with a historiography, Christian and Jewish, that has in its quest for origins long adopted the genealogical methods of the fifteenth-century polemicist. Like the "Antiquarian historian" of Nietzsche's second "Untimely meditation," the historian of Spain and its Jews too often "greets the soul of his nation across the long dark centuries of confusion as his own soul." The preceding pages are about the history of lineage and the history of history in fifteenth-century Sepharad. But they are just as much about these shades of genealogy that have proved so difficult to exorcize from our own historical practices.[31]

Continued interrogation of our own pedagogy, our own research, and our own writing remain in order, whether or not we still have any hopes or pretensions of "liberating" ourselves or others thereby. Cultural studies, among other things, is about the idea that just as text is never a second, more ideal order of reality, so, too, we are never "above" what we are studying, teaching, discussing, writing. Rather than fix on a supposedly delimited time and space as the guarantor of the purest approach to truth, let us be aware that we are constantly tacking between two formations of identity, the one (the notion of "ourselves") inescapable for continued human life and being continually reshaped and nurtured by the other (the "past" in its relics), and attend to our work as not simply the *knowing* but rather the active *making* or *performance* of history. Maybe in that way, rather than be ultimately tempted to conclude that the question of any profound commonalities among Jews through time and space is a trick of the present, we will allow ourselves to remain humbled—not hobbled—by Paul Gilroy's reminder that "the fragile psychological, emotional, and cultural correspondences which connect diaspora populations in spite of their manifest differences are often apprehended only fleetingly and in ways that persistently confound the protocols of academic orthodoxy."[32]

3

Seasons and Lifetimes

For the next half-hour or so, I will be speaking of things that matter to all of us but, ultimately, that none of us really understands very well. My theme throughout these few reflections is this: at every stage, everyone's career is embedded, try as we might to forget it or to escape it, within the web of relations to ancestors and descendants, biological as well as rhetorical.

Let that brief statement, that topic sentence, bind together these "reflections," a term that, if you don't know it already, serves primarily to dignify what are otherwise random thoughts and vignettes, each of which seems somehow significant but whose connections to one another are not yet, and may never be, entirely clear.

In any case, my topic is a broad one. Fortunately, I happen to be at a point in my own career that affords me the luxury of focusing my life and thoughts, at least briefly, on such an ambitious theme. And so one day recently I sat for a long first coffee in midtown Manhattan with a new acquaintance who is beginning a book on the intertwined characters of Christianity, Judaism, and Islam, especially as they relate to the problem of political liberalism. Knowing that he was himself a religious skeptic, to say the least, in the course of our conversation I confessed, a bit nervously, that I have a sentimental attraction to the Hasidim, those rigorously observant Jews who are distinctive in their dress and carefully maintain the boundaries of their own communities.

"Why?" he asked. "Is it because life out here in America seems to be overly transient, too burdened with disconnected images from a million different sources, lacking in meaning, desperately overreliant on material possessions?"—or words to similar effect.

"Yeah," I said, "that's it! Somehow it seems to me that I have to struggle constantly to balance between autonomy and connectedness, and somehow it seems to me that they don't."

Let me clarify again, then, that when I speak of the problem of representing our ancestors, I do not imagine for a moment that it is possible or desirable, certainly not now, for the problematic limits of personal identity to be resolved through a decision to live your life *as if you were your own ancestor*—or to raise your children as if they should become you.

Alexis de Tocqueville, writing in the nineteenth century, claimed that this kind of merger was the norm, presumably even without conscious effort, in traditional societies where "families stay in the same situation, and frequently in the same place, for centuries. This, so to speak, renders all the generations contemporary."[1] I have always imagined that here, Tocqueville was thinking particularly of agricultural societies, and that somehow the succession of birth, new generation, aging, and death was thereby akin to the cycle of plowing, raising, and harvesting crops. It has a kind of timeless appeal; it seems a kind of timeless ideal. But it is worth remembering that this kind of "natural" ideal was also part and parcel of what Marx called "the idiocy of rural life."[2]

How, then, without erasing our precious sense of uniqueness and without hiding the terrible fact of our aloneness, can we articulate our own life's careers not only with the cycle of generations—parents and children, grandparents and grandchildren, and so on—but also with the cycle of seasons that, as we know but as needs to be said explicitly, today cannot be taken for granted but whose preservation becomes our own responsibility? To begin to address that question, let us turn back to the middle of the last century, to the time when a serious, professional anthropologist might be equally concerned with the origins of the human species as with its situation today. There once was a wonderful teacher who exemplified those concerns, and his name was Loren Eiseley.

Eiseley used to write haunting essays in which his own voice powerfully evoked the lonely situation of each and every human being, trying to figure out how, in language, to be separate and connected at the same time, as in this passage from his 1970 book *The Invisible Pyramid*:

In the year 1910 Halley's comet—the comet that among many visitations had flared in 1066 over the Norman invasion of England—was again brightening the night skies of earth.

Like hundreds of other little boys of the new century, I was held up in my father's arms under the cottonwoods of a cold and leafless spring to see the hurtling emissary of the void. My father told me something then that is one of my earliest and most cherished memories.

"If you live to be an old man," he said carefully, fixing my eyes on the midnight spectacle, "you will see it again. It will come back in seventy-five years. Remember," he whispered in my ear, "I will be gone, but you will see it. All that time it will be traveling in the dark, but somewhere, far out there"—he swept a hand toward the blue horizon of the planet—"it will turn back. It is running glittering through millions of miles."

I tightened my hold on my father's neck and stared uncomprehendingly at the heavens. Once more he spoke against my ear and for us two alone. "Remember, all you have to do is to be careful and wait. You will be seventy-eight or seventy-nine years old. I think you will live to see it—for me," he whispered a little sadly with the foreknowledge that was part of his nature.

"Yes, Papa," I said dutifully, having little or no grasp of seventy-five years or millions of miles on the floorless pathways of space. Nevertheless I was destined to recall the incident all my life. It was out of love for a sad man who clung to me as I to him that, young though I was, I remembered. There are long years still to pass, and already I am breathing like a tired runner, but the voice still sounds in my ears and I know with the sureness of maturity that the great wild satellite has reversed its course and is speeding on its homeward journey toward the sun.[3]

Why does this anecdote evoke such a powerful ache in me, as I suspect it does in at least some of you? Here, at least, is one question I think we *can* answer, just by spending a few minutes looking closely at a few of the phrases that Eiseley wrote:

First: "Like hundreds of little boys of the new century." Look what happens in this one sentence. The old man we see on the cover of the book, just by saying "I" of a little boy sixty years earlier, sweeps us back to cross in a single line of text what by then was already half a century, and he reminds us by contrast that as the aging man writes, the promising and disastrous twentieth century is itself growing old.

Second: the linkage between "the cottonwoods of a cold and leafless spring" and the "void" beyond them, a lesson that not only every winter but also every day that the new green shoots are delayed reminds us that the renewal of life is never to be taken for granted.

Third: "If you live to be an old man," an early reminder, perhaps more shattering even than Eiseley acknowledges here, of a parent's mortality.

Fourth: the father's whispered wish that his son see Halley's Comet the next time, "for me," as if to say, "live long—and remember me always," and the weight of a promise "dutifully" made long ago, with little comprehension at the time it was made that the promise was not necessarily the boy's to keep.

And finally, or at any rate last for now—since I have no wish to exhaust the meanings of this extraordinary passage—the relation between the predictability of the universe, known "with the sureness of maturity," and the aging author's doubt of his own personal constancy, an old-fashioned term that sounds like it means permanence but really means loyalty.

But before leaving this anecdote, a footnote or maybe better a bit of a sequel: because I will, next summer, take up what is somewhat euphemistically called a "permanent position" in (of all places) the state of Kansas—not so far from Lincoln, Nebraska, where Eiseley was born and hence where his father held him to see the comet and enjoined him to see it again—I have been reading William Least Heat-Moon's *PrairyErth* (1991), a patiently detailed natural and human history of a sparsely populated county in that oh-so-central state. Introducing his portrait of one of the county's oldest residents, Blanche Swilling, the author writes: "She was outside late last night to watch the comet again, and she says, *It isn't much now, not what it was in 1910.*" And that's all he says about the comet—almost as if he were counting on me to come along, at this point in my own odd and unpredictable trajectory, between my first reading of Eiseley and my own arrival in Kansas, and find the particular resonance in hearing of another who had, indeed, lived to see the comet twice. It is certainly pertinent to add that if Blanche Swilling was less impressed by the comet's second appearance in her lifetime, it was not necessarily because she had become jaded or her eyes had dimmed: the far greater amount of ambient electric light, in rural Kansas as in great cities, likely dimmed the cosmic impression made by the comet's return.

In any case, surely in this moment with his father lies a key to what makes so much of Loren Eiseley's writings extraordinary—albeit in a manner echoed by others concerned with the interplay of deep time and human time, such as William Least Heat-Moon. I would identify that quality as the ability to link his own voice to that of all human generations, not just his own lineage but also the entire species, and not only backward, but forward as well. Elsewhere Eiseley writes of wandering through the ruins of a great city and describes finding himself in front of a shattered store window, with precious stones still scattered inside, and seeing to his saddened puzzlement the intact skeletal forearm of a woman in front of the window—until he is brought out of this reverie by the voice of his wife: "Honey, how do you think it looks on me?" The little boy grown old, remembering his father so many years before, linking the time of his personal memory to the cosmic sequences of the departure and return of the comet, was able perhaps by that token to keep in mind, without shattering his mind, that we too will someday be relics at best.

Fathers, as the Eiseley anecdote tells us as well, are complicated things. They are scary, more often than we care to acknowledge. They can be useful, too. And there are many kinds of fathers. There's a phrase in German, *Doktorvater*. It refers to the close and consequential relationship doctoral candidates in the German universities traditionally had with their advisors, who were in a position to make or break their students' subsequent careers. Eiseley had a *Doktorvater*, too, an anthropologist of an earlier generation named Frank Speck.

My own *Doktorvater*, the anthropologist Stanley Diamond, I did not know so well, and yet he taught me much, for he, too, was concerned with the links among the individual, the group, and the natural world, and the ways those articulations had changed over time. For Diamond, the critical term of anthropology was *primitive*, and the key message of his own life's career was that some essential wisdom of our primitive ancestors has been lost in civilization. Diamond wrote, of the ritual dramas that, as he said, "cluster around life crises or discontinuities, either of the individual or of the group at large," that they display "an apparent continuity from the individual's setting in the group to the group's setting in nature."[4]

But Stanley Diamond did not mean to evoke a primitive Eden. In thus describing how primitive people addressed their own awareness of mortality, both sudden and cyclical, both individual and collective, he did not mean to suggest that primitive persons were never afraid, just that they knew how to address their fears together and to address them in the world. Neither, by suggesting that individuals related to the group as the group related to the natural world, did he mean that the family was ever simply the individual writ large (nor, for that matter, is the ethnic group ever merely the family writ large).

At any rate we are not, by Diamond's definition, primitives; instead, Diamond warned us—rather shrilly, it might seem, and without some of the resigned grace that Loren Eiseley possessed, that "our rationalized, mechanized and secularized civilization tends to produce standard, modal persons rather than natural variety. The individual is always in danger of dissolving into the function or the status."[5] Diamond is saying that we tend to confuse ourselves with the social roles we play, so that, for example, I may be unduly anxious about the strange question whether it is Jonathan who is coming to speak to you, with results that we cannot predict but nevertheless welcome; or rather Jonathan who must adequately appear in the role of "speaker," according to some preexisting script that must be divined as best as possible in advance.

Diamond was thinking primarily of bureaucratic roles that individuals assume in civilization—teacher, politician, parent, cop— but he was worried too about the danger of his contemporaries slipping into ethnic identity roles, trying to make themselves fit some preexisting notion of what a member of a given group should be and do. He cautioned me more than once against going, as it were, too far "inside" my own supposed ethnic identity, of imagining, I suppose, that I was Jewish because it was somehow better to be Jewish than not. He imposed a very high standard, that is, on anyone who wants to make a life's career out of the performance of a particular group identity. And yet, as I have said, he mourned the isolation of the civilized individual, from both genealogy and nature.

Hence a dilemma: How is it possible to respond to the materiality of being the representative of the ancestors in the present? How, as it were, is it possible to keep faith, like the old man Loren Eiseley had become remembering his boyhood promise to his father? How is it possible to attend to this imperative without effacing what is particular to one's own story, one's own makeup, and at the same time without shrinking one's efforts at shared identification from the entirety of the species, to the limits of one's own group? And how do we evaluate the resources for such an effort in our time? Is it harder to respond to in America now than it was in previous generations? Do we have fewer resources for doing so than previous generations did?

What are the consequences, for example, of no longer being able to speak or read the same language our great-grandparents spoke, even for the purpose of arguing with them in our own minds? What are the consequences of regaining competence in that ancestral tongue? Let me just suggest that this is something that can in fact be done, and although its consequences are unpredictable, they are well worth the effort. I quote a snippet from a poem by Diana Der-Hovanessian, quoted in turn by the anthropologist Michael Fischer in his essay on "Ethnography and the Postmodern Arts of Memory."[6] The poem is titled "Learning an Ancestral Tongue":

> My ancestors talk
> to me in dangling
> myths.
> Each word a riddle
> each dream
> heirless.

On sunny days
I bury words.
They put out roots
and coil around
forgotten syntax.
Next spring a full
blown anecdote
will sprout.

This poem brings me round, in turn, to a term I spent at Dartmouth College, at the School of Criticism and Theory, in the terribly hot summer of 1988. Fellow students organized a poetry reading one evening whose highlight in my memory was Gline Griffiths's Caribbean lament about elite theory, including the complaint "dey put Descartes before dey horse" and concluding in frustration, "cogito ergo damn!" My contribution to that evening was a translation into Yiddish of the snippet from the Der-Hovanessian poem that I just quoted. The Yiddish (in transliteration and in the "original" Hebrew alphabet) goes like this:

mayne ovos un mayne emahos
darshenen far mir kh'veys-vos
yedes vort a retenish
yeder kholem
on a yoyresh.
az s'iz sheyn in droysn
bagrob ikh verter.
zey vortslen zikh ayn
un viklen zikh arum
a fargesenem sintaks.
vesnetsayt vet zikh tsebliyen
a zaftike maysele.

מײנע אבות און מײנע אמהות
דרשענען פֿאַר מיר כ'ווייס-וואָס
יעדעס וואָרט א רעטעניש
יעדער חלום
אָן א יורש
אז ס'איז שײן אין דרויסן
באַגראַב איך ווערטער
זיי וואָרצלען זיך אײן
און וויקלען זיך ארום
א פֿאַרגעסענעם סינטאַקס
וועסנעצײט וועט זיך צעבליִען
א זאָפֿטיקע מעסהלע

The possibility of reading a poem in Yiddish at the School of Criticism and Theory may serve to indicate that in some ways we now have *more* resources for reweaving a text of generations than, let us say, were available when the little Loren Eiseley first saw Halley's comet. Thus, through the Internet, I now know a third cousin who lives in Israel. His great-grandfather and mine were brothers. However, his great-grandfather was the only one of the siblings who never left Russia, and, to my knowledge, links with that branch of the family were broken from the time of the Russian Revolution until just a few months ago. I had, however, long ago heard about our common ancestor, my great-great-grandfather Shimon Boyarin, and knew that he had been a rural dairyman. Over twenty years ago, in fact, while I was first studying Yiddish, I had a dream that I was standing on the edge of a field. An elderly Jew with a white beard stood in the field, pouring milk into an old-fashioned jug. As I watched him, he looked up at me, smiled, and waved.

But outside that dream, I had never seen his face—until recently, when Dmitri Boyarer mailed me a photograph of our common great-great-grandfather, and I was struck by his resemblance to my brother Daniel. Such resemblances are, of course, the stuff of family gatherings, and there is something very striking about them. But if I were to stress them too much here, I would be guilty of the greatest sin in the academic humanities today—the sin known as "essentialism."

"Essentialism," to oversimplify, is speaking as if a thing is adequately described by a given name we might ascribe to it—to say, for example, that "women are thus and thus," and therefore to suppose that any woman, any proper woman, is "thus and thus." But it does not only refer to the stereotyping of others; it can also be a strategy by which one asserts one's own belonging to a certain group and the right to speak as a member of that group. Whether it refers to descriptions of others or assertions about oneself, part of the reason that academics are skeptical of essentialism is that it seems to cut against the core liberal value of each person's uniqueness and to substitute collective attributions for both individual responsibility and the group's obligation to respect that individual. In that sense, if only somewhat tenuously, our suspicion of essentialism is linked to Stanley Diamond's concern about the threat that the civilized person might dissolve into the set of roles that he or she occupies in society.

Harking back to the Old Country, as I have been doing, might suggest that I view our great-grandparents as still somehow primitives, still somehow free from the tension between autonomy and connectedness that I've been trying to evoke. Of course, no such thing is the case. The individual was not discovered in America. And I am not speaking only of an individualism that is necessarily linked to the Enlightenment, or to modern secularism. Some two hundred years ago, the Hasidic master Menachem Mendl Morgenstern, known as the Kotsker Rebbe after the name of the central Polish town where he held court, became one of the luminaries of that movement to which today's Hasidim, those whom I described earlier in this talk as seeming somehow to exemplify freedom from the dilemma of the separate individual who wants to be connected without losing himself. Far from standing as a bulwark of tradition, far from inspiring loyal preservation of the ways of the ancestors as against the winds of change, the Kotsker Rebbe already stressed in his teachings the central role of individual consciousness and the need to struggle with all one's strength against the tendency of worship to slip into a rote practice. Young men streamed to join him from all over Poland, and they stayed with him as long as they could, placing real strains on the very family structure that was the bedrock of the continuing Jewish community.

Indeed, becoming old was a problem for the Kotsker Rebbe, as Professor Abraham Joshua Heschel writes in his book about that tormented and enigmatic figure:

> When a person grows old and he is losing his strength, the only thing that's left for him as far as worship goes is: either to imitate what others do or to imitate himself, to imitate what he used to do.
>
> But Kotsk holds that one may not imitate the other and one may not imitate himself. Imitation is false. Therefore one is forbidden to be old. And the problem is that people grow old while still young. Kotsk claimed that freshness stands higher than piety. The older the colder; what's newer is truer. What is holy comes unexpected.[7]

Of course, no one can really forbid us to grow old. And of course, our old people are treasures in ways that we barely recognize. Maybe, if the Kotsker's saying that "one is forbidden to be old" has a message for us, it is rather that, when we grow old, we must not forbid our descendants from exercising the right to be young, to let what is holy arrive, unexpected.

When we grow old, the young with whom we identify remember for us, as it were, our youth. But this kind of magic transference can only happen through and with language. It is important to remember that what makes the relation among generations in any way a cycle, rather than merely a sequence (so that, for example, a grandmother can recall her own youth in the image of a granddaughter), is language, as is evidenced in the first instance in the practice of giving infants names that refer back to ancestors. The purest form of invoking past generations in the new is when grandchildren are named for their grandparents. The French scholar Pierre Legendre illustrates this notion of identification through generations by reference to a Greek inscription, evidently on a family tomb, that marks the names of "Philocles son of Dikaios [and of *his* son], Dikaios son of Philocles." As Legendre summarizes:

> Each name is declined twice, once in the nominative and once in the genitive. The same grammatical operation repeats itself, but the names are inverted. For each deceased, the quality of sonship comes first. Nevertheless, there is neither equal status nor reciprocal position: the first name mentioned is the only one which presents the same person, whom it presents, in the juxtaposition of sequences, in the double quality of son and father: Philocles is son of his father [the elder Dikaios, who is not represented on the grave stele] and father of his son. The other name [that is, the name Dikaios] presents two persons, the grandfather and the grandson.[8]

A more simple, and perhaps more easily understood, analogy to this practice is the memory I will always bear of my own grandfather—great-great-grandfather Shimon's grandson, great-grandfather Mordkhe's youngest son, my father Sidney's father, Yisroel, whom I just called "Grandpa"—calling me "little Grandpa."

Now I do not mean, in focusing exclusively on patronymics here, to suggest that the process of extending personal identity through the repetition of naming across generations is something particular to maleness. At the same time, if, as I am trying gently to suggest, it remains a potentially useful resource for being in the world, it should be amenable not only to recuperation but to reinvention as well, in ways that take into account our own desire to reimagine gender.

Moreover, to point to the ways that generations of grandparents and grandchildren can be brought to identify with each other is not necessarily to solve the other question I raised—how we can acquire a strong group identity without at the same time, so to speak, disidentifying with the rest of the species. Precisely this problem is bravely and effectively evoked in a recent film called *Hiding and Seeking*, by Menachem Daum, an Orthodox Jew living in Brooklyn. In this film, Daum, a child and son-in-law of Holocaust survivors and the father of two sons who are full-time adult Talmud students in Israel, takes those sons on a journey back to the towns in Poland where their grandparents had lived. We learn, in scenes shot prior to the trip, that Daum's father-in-law thinks Daum should not follow through with the plan of attempting to locate the Polish peasant family who, at great risk to themselves, had hidden the father-in-law for more than two years during World War II; and we likewise hear Daum's sons speaking in stark terms of their conviction that, "essentially" if I may say so, all Poles are anti-Semites and there is little to be gained in a search for the good ones. This documentary film turns out to have an extraordinarily dramatic plot, so I don't want to speak about it too much. So here, at least at the beginning of the film, even though it would seem that the grandfather and grandsons share a profound devotion to what we are used to calling their "culture," this commonality does not seem to afford them an openness toward the contingency of the world, the holiness that comes unexpected, but instead merely to reinforce a skeptical mistrust of "all the *goyim*." The film suggests too, however, that such a narrowing of group identity might itself be a kind of continued hiding, which could be healed, rather than reinforced, by a renewal of the sense of continuity of generations, as in the moment when, wandering through a half-abandoned Polish rural graveyard looking for the filmmaker's great-grandparents' tombs, one of his sons suddenly cries, "Dad, I found her!" Not: I found the grave, but rather—here she is, my great-great-grandmother.

Loren Eiseley did not, in fact, live to see Halley's Comet again. Perhaps his father should have said to him, "Or if not you, then your own child someday to be born." I'm sorry now to say that I must not have attended to it myself, the last time it passed our way. The great wild satellite is rushing away from us, right now. But certainly some of us must remember seeing it, and we cannot help but hope that our children or grandchildren, if not we, will see it again. Perhaps recuperation and reinvention of an identification across the cycle of generations can help us to discern the possibility of a freedom that is not egocentric, and in turn do more to assure that our descendants will indeed live to see the next coming. At any rate, that future is not now. The most important thing is to remember, as nearly always as possible, how brief is our own passage of consciousness between one oblivion and another, how little we possess, how much we share and how much we have to pass on.

4

Toward an Anthropology of the Twentieth Century

To Professor Edward Said, of blessed memory

When Leslie Morris so generously invited me to speak at this conference, I almost instantaneously provided her with the tentative title "Toward an Anthropology of the Twentieth Century." Of course, the twentieth century remains an awkward designation. It is split, from one perspective, between "before" and "after" the defining cataclysm of World War II and its attendant genocide. Moreover, it is not clear, yet, that it is best understood as an epoch ending with the fall of the Soviet Union. Even less clear is that the attack on the Twin Towers, whose seductive proximity to the new millennium exerts a powerful historical magnetism, indicates a tectonic shift into a new era. Rather, when I referred to the twentieth century, I was thinking, to put it in the most prosaic terms I can, of our situation, today, yesterday, and at every moment between 1932 and the time, if it comes, when we collectively determine how to share this planet instead of burning it up.

Let me echo once again, as it seems I will do my whole life as part of the quest for critically effective speech, Benjamin's "Theses on the Philosophy of History": The pile of ruins continues to grow at our feet. Now, however, we must understand that it includes not only human ash and the ruins of cities (we should not have been shocked to discover that those ruined cities would include our own) but literally our garbage as well—the kind of thing archaeologists love these days, along with the ruin of the long-stored petroleum energy that is our heritage from earlier geological ages. What I was hoping to do was to begin to articulate, though I am probably capable only of alluding to it, the question of how critical thought is limited by the assumptions that our species can and must survive. In this respect, the term *anthropology* is therefore to be understood as the study of the conditions of possibility of continued human life.

After so much study of the poetics and politics of the memory of Nazi genocide in the last few decades, it seems odd to say it, but it seems to me that it remains very difficult for us to talk or think coherently about extinction and memory at the same time. This might have something to do with the fact that (and I speak somewhat speculatively now) in Jewish discourse, if not Western religious discourse more generally, the possibility of ultimate extinction, of the Jews or of humanity tout court, seems to be a taboo concept, rigorously absent even from our eschatologies.

I really do invite debate on this point, by the way, both because it seems an important one that has not been considered, and because the first person I mentioned it to, Susannah Heschel, immediately contradicted it by pointing to the hymn "Adon Olam" (Master of the Universe) that Jewish congregations sing every week at the end of Sabbath services. For "Adon Olam" contains the phrase, "And after all has ceased to be, He will reign, alone and awesome." And lonely?

In this respect, as Jack Kugelmass and others have pointed out,[1] genocide in Europe stands not only as an epochal event, but also as our closest collective encounter with annihilation. We will continue talking of it as long as there is breath within us, and each conversation will be an event in itself. Just three weeks ago, during the Sabbath of the intermediate days of Passover, I attended a conference whose theme and occasion both resonate with this one. The conference, "Contested Memories of the Holocaust," was held in conjunction with a seminar on the cultural memory of Nazi genocide that has been conducted jointly this spring, via videoconference, at Dartmouth College and at Tel Aviv University.

One of the first speakers, Froma Zeitlin from Princeton, spoke about the journeys, by now often highly ritualized, that American and Israeli Jews take to the sites of their ancestral homes in Europe. She brought along a bit of show-and-tell, the one souvenir, of all the *tshatshkes* now available for tourists in the Polish city of Lublin, that she thought worthwhile retrieving: a torn fragment from a Torah scroll. She reported the response of a Jewish friend when she brought it back home: "You should bury it." After all, that is what we do with a scrap of sacred text we can no longer use. "But," reports Froma, "I said, 'No, I'm keeping it.'"

Later in the day, thinking about Froma's fragment, the notion popped into my mind that it would be meet to take it and read from it—whatever is legible in it, whatever seemingly random passages of the Torah it might bear—on one of our days of mourning, presumably the Ninth of Av, when we commemorate the destruction of the Temple. But I know that this would be in itself a form of ritual violence, if not an impossibility, since a Torah scroll that is in any way illegible or incomplete—a scroll, that is, that might not convey perfectly its own literal nature as a simulacrum of uncorrupted memory—is one that cannot be read from in public, but must remain shut up inside the ark.

To phrase the dilemma this way would seem to imply that the archaeological artifact is somehow a truer token of memory than the scroll intact, cyclically scanned each year, completed every Simchas Torah only to be flipped over and begun anew. But of course Froma's presentation of the scrap at the Contested Memories conference was itself a kind of new ritual act, the irruption of the fragment immediately absorbed within a revised commemorative framework.

We are not comfortable with these uncanny fragments out of context, and seem to seek always to reset them, though we know or should know that an easy assumption of a strict correlation between proximity and authenticity should be questioned. The question is not only the very status, or place of an origin, but also the impulse even when we doubt the solidity of origins somehow to return to them. It is an impulse I know well and have displayed in my own emblems: *From a Ruined Garden, Storm from Paradise,* the echoes between which I never noticed—honest—before thinking about what I might say to you today. It is an impulse I have also known when playing my own version of the game we can call, "Where would you be if money were no object?" to which my answer is: inside a little study house made out of wood, in the midst of a garden, with the words carved in Hebrew above the entrance: *"v'ets hakhayim besokh hagan"*—and the Tree of Life was within the garden.

Of course, I don't live there, you don't live in a garden either, and we all do know that. We are so inured, in fact, to the distance from origins that it is something like the opposite that appears more likely to seduce us: the fetishization of loss. Adam Phillips has recently described the pleasures inherent in the child's discovery of what Freud called the *fort-da* game, making things go away and reappear again. Freud had described, in *Beyond the Pleasure Principle,* the child's pleasure in throwing a reel tied to a string over the edge of its cot, and then pulling it back so he could see it again, as "related to the child's great cultural achievement—the instinctual renunciation . . . which he had made in allowing his mother to go away without protesting. He compensated himself for this, as it were, by himself staging the disappearance and return of the objects within his reach."[2] Phillips glosses Freud's investigation thus: "What is it inside us, Freud seems to be wondering, that can turn an absence into a pleasurably open space, that makes an improvisation out of a deprivation?"[3]

I think you will not disagree that our investigations of memory and exile, no matter how intellectually rigorous, also come with substantial and inevitable psychic engagement, a kaleidoscope of projections upon and reactions against the dead, ranging from obsessive longing to revulsion. Unstable as the dynamics of distancing and identification may be, for the sake of our own freedom we cannot refrain from trying to understand these dynamics as we shape and practice them, and from trying to achieve a relation to our dead that leaves us at least not cripplingly burdened either by a sense that we are exploiting them or by a sense that we are idolizing them.

In a somewhat different register, some of our colleagues might wonder whether, if not perversely taking pleasure in the abyssal loss of Nazi genocide, we are not inclined to take an overly improvisatory approach to the memories of victimhood. Not so much to refute them, but rather because our tentative explorations of the poetics of loss are so vitally urgent, I would like to see whether it helps further to focus our thinking and our discussions somewhat to resist the vectors of space and time, away from a central or originary Europe and toward our own present. Such a strategy might also help us to remember, against the aggressive use of the term *presentism* as an invective meant to inoculate objects of study supposedly distant in time and space from our own more transient interests, that what we might in turn call "pastism" or even "there-ism" is also a charged and contingent construct. One way to help bring "past-ism" and "there-ism" more clearly to consciousness is to reread Johannes Fabian's *Time and the Other* (1983), a lucid critique of the rhetorical construction of temporal *cordons sanitaires*. Another way to do this is to set forth by contrast tokens, even in the form of vignettes, that may help us to suppose instead of an absence a co-presence—contemporaneous with the disaster in Europe, but at a distance from it in America; or alternatively, still in Europe, but many years later.

I will move us briefly away, that is, only to remind us who and where we are now, and how much depends on how and what we remember. Famously, Benjamin locates messianic energy in the memory of enslaved ancestors, not the dream of liberated grandchildren. But this does not mean that Benjamin escapes the poetic necessity of descent, of generation, of continuity, since after all, there are no ancestors without descendants, even if, for a time after disaster, there may be an excess of ancestors, a dearth of descendants, as the Parish Yiddish poet Moshe Szulsztein wrote in his epic *Baym pinkes fun Lublin* (Before the Chronicle of Lublin):

> *es veln nisht feln*
> *di nemen nokh vemen*
>
> *There will be no lack*
> *Of ancestors to name children after.*

Maybe this proximity to the unthinkability of collective extinction, of the extinction of the Name, the Word, in short, the end of memory, also lies behind the rhetorical coercion in the first line of the first poem in the first book published by the great Yiddish writer Chaim Grade after the war's end. The book is titled *Yo!* (Yes!), and its first line is the starkly imperative *Yidishe mames, hot kinder!* Jewish mothers, have children!

In the words of these Yiddish poets we can see, now, something of a rush to replacement, an anxiety of absence, that only gradually, and only for some, was in its turn displaced by a poetics of loss. It takes time for mourning to take its shape.

That process of "taking shape" is, I understand, the subject of this conference. I note that each element of this conference's title, and the seminar out of which it grew, is a figure of distance, whether spatial or temporal: "out of Europe," "since 1945," "memory," "exile." Let's see whether an attempt to articulate, as a counterpoint, *presence*, will help us to understand better what it means to be gathered around those words, here at Madison, on April 29, 2004.

I can think of two commonsense contrasts to being removed from a primary event in both time and space. One is to set ourselves back in, or nearer to, the time of that event, but at a different place. Here I begin by citing Wallace Markfield's wonderful novel *Teitlebaum's Window*, a hilariously and heartbreakingly intimate account of growing up Jewish in Brighton Beach in the 1930s, told largely in the form of the child narrator's diary entries. I'll give just two:

> April 6, 1938.
> No teacher did too much today as it was the last day before the Easter Week vacation.
> We got a big letter from one of Dad's relatives in Europe. She is a girl who wants to go to America, if we could help. Mom said this is from a part of dad's family that when I was born didn't even send a mazeltoff.[4]

The second excerpt is part of a note written to the narrator by his mother, dated September 9, 1941. She is awaiting delivery of a new refrigerator, and she makes plans to describe its arrival in a phone call with the narrator—but in code, lest the spiteful Uncle Phillie know of her new acquisition:

> And as I know you will be waiting for my news when you call your dad with his current-events head has set up the following arrangements.
> If you hear me say I'm upset France didn't fight a little harder it means the refrigerator came, it's a reconditioned model but I had no strength anymore to argue with the landlord.

If you here me say Sad news from the Polish corridor it means they had trouble getting it through my door.

If you hear me say The lights are going out all over Europe it means I plugged it in and right away the fuse blew.

If you hear me say I'm very very sorry for what they did to Holland it means they got it so filthy I had to go over the whole thing with Dutch Cleanser.[5]

It is impossible to comment very clearly on Wallace Markfield's own awareness of an absence, in this novel that he published in 1970, of almost any representation of the particular Jewish disaster that was taking place by September 9, 1941, unless by pointing to the understated but unmistakable desperation that echoes from the pages—untranscribed, in Markfield's novel—of the "big letter" received from a distant relative in 1938, and to the equally unmistakable, if still implicit, acknowledgment that the failure of the narrator's parents to respond to such desperation is explained by nothing more than a grossly misplaced sense of outraged reciprocity. It does seem that, now at least, it would take a good deal of moral courage for a novelist to set down with such exquisite wit this evidence of what we cannot help read as a nearly damning obliviousness. Especially striking in the latter passage is its repeated invocation of the names of nations—France, Poland, Holland—along with the name Europe that encompasses them all. As Benedict Anderson has reminded us, "current events," conveyed in those decades by the radio, helped to bring nations together, so this passage seems strikingly apt for this Bildungsroman that marks growth toward adulthood as a move away from the local and Jewish toward the global and American, and actually ends with the narrator's induction into the armed forces of the United States.

Sherwin Nuland's memoir of his immigrant father, *Lost in America*, continues (in a very different register) the narrative where Markfield's leaves off. Throughout this account his father's own troubled distance from the narrating child is echoed by a poverty of detail about the father's lost home in Eastern Europe. What I want to focus on here, however, is the depiction of his father suddenly somehow confronting, it seems for the first time, the destruction of his hometown, Novoselitz:

> One evening early in 1947 was like none that had ever preceded it. At about 6:00 p.m., he suddenly flung himself into the small entrance foyer of the apartment, almost falling. He was clutching a crumpled and disarrayed copy of the *Jewish Daily Forward* in his upraised hand, as if to indicate the cause of the tears streaming down his face, which was contorted with grief. As the heavy door slammed shut behind him, he slapped the newspaper against his leg in an expression of hopeless desolation, crying out the immensity of his sorrow to the heavens, to each of us and to no one, all at once. For some moments, it was impossible to know what shattering stroke of despair had torn so deeply into him that it called up such wellsprings of lamentation. He stood there virtually hysterical, unable to form comprehensible words . . . Only gradually did he return to a full awareness of everything around him. In flat, halting sentences, the entire horrifying narrative emerged [of the day on which] [e]very Jew in Novoselitz was murdered.[6]

Where do we place this passage in a sequence of event and memory? One option would be to identify not so much the father's experience on reading the newspaper as the author's consciousness in setting down this scene half a century later, as an instance of what Marianne Hirsch calls post-memory, the reworked and formulated matter of an ancestor's experience as an element of personal history. More to the point, I think that the setting of this passage confounds any lucid sequencing of event and memory: It is liminal, at the "edge" of that time, or as we more commonly say, "just after 1945." It is a newspaper account, yet not contemporaneous with the event it describes. This passage suggests to me rather that there are certain scenes—here, Nuland's father's reaction to the newspaper account in *Forverts*—

that, albeit distanced from what we might think of as some primary historical datum (here, the actual massacre at Novoselitz), are better likened to ripples in a pond, each one at once an echo and an event in itself, the most recent and, as it were, widest ripple being the moment just now when I read this passage to you, and your no doubt sensational, that is, visceral reaction to the scene.

But it is not only in such calamitous confrontations of awareness that the supposedly natural sequence of loss followed by memory is disrupted, reversed or confounded in more complex ways. Losses, as I think we know but as still seems contrary to common sense, keep happening. Just a few weeks ago, a friend from Paris called to report the following: Her aging father had had a dream the previous night. In the dream, he received, completely unexpected of course, a phone call from a brother lost in World War II. The brother reported in the dream that he had survived the war, that he was doing well, and that he had a family of his own. But when my friend's dreaming father wanted to reply, the phone connection went dead and he was unable to call his brother back.

The complement, I suppose, to being at a different place at the same time is being in the same place—what we are calling "Europe"—at a different time. Twenty years ago, on my first and only trip to Poland, my colleague Jack Kugelmass entrusted me with a mission. Jack was curating the first exhibition, mounted at the YIVO Institute, of Monika Krajewski's photographs of Jewish cemeteries in Poland. How extraordinary it was, in February 1984, in a Warsaw still depressed in the wake of martial law, to come into Monika and her husband Staszek's apartment and be warmed by their account of what was then the very first stirring of a reimagining of the possibility of Jewish community in Poland. How dramatic was the contrast between those meetings and my travels, just a few days later, with a Jewish Federation Young

Leadership group from Westchester County stopping in Poland briefly before rushing off to Israel. So hurried were those missionaries that they did not have time to see both the death camp at Auschwitz and also Kazimierz, the Jewish quarter of Krakow, and to my distress but not my surprise chose to see where the Jews had died rather than where the Jews had lived.

Monika and Staszek, and others like them, have nevertheless stayed in Poland, and we recently received the following report of the bar mitzvah of their second son, Daniel:

> Daniel's bar mitzvah on January 10, 2004, was probably the first bar mitzvah of a Down Syndrome boy in Poland, ever. It was a wonderful experience to all the numerous friends present in the Warsaw Nozyk synagogue. We invented a non-standard but meaningful modification of the routine, with Rabbi Schudrich's full support and participation. Daniel was almost 14 then, and very eager and proud to have the bar mitzvah. . . . The shul was full, a very unusual view. . . .
>
> Daniel showed and explained the large paintings on Biblical themes that he had made for the occasion. . . . The explanation was partly in words, and partly in gestures, bordering on a pantomime.
>
> Daniel was at ease and radiated so much happiness that a colleague—a regular member of the synagogue minyan—said that to him this was the most memorable event ever in this synagogue; another friend said that David's voice was like that of the High Priest. . . .
>
> We said a few words from the bimah, also [our older son] Gabriel, himself a punk, acknowledged Daniel's involvement, not matched by his own. His friends were present, too, a colorful company, with dreadlocks and mohawks. . . .
>
> Here are some photos taken by Monika on another day (what happened on that Shabbat must be kept only in our memories).

Shabbat, of course, cannot be mechanically reproduced, and here at any rate is one set of practicing Jewish parents, living in Poland, who will catch the allusion and may well have had it in mind. I will not comment further, except to underscore the extraordinary generosity and resilience in matters of generation and identity to which this letter testifies.

It is good when a gift like this letter from the Krajewskis arrives, unexpected. So much else seems to conspire to discourage us, even to pervert the seeming innocence of pleasant and private nostalgic memories, the kind I experience, for example, when I borrow or rent a car and drive around the Northeast listening to WCBS-FM, the oldies station, as its jingle used to run, "you sing along to." Lately my private retreats into nostalgia, at least those portions spent driving near Newark Airport on the New Jersey Turnpike, have been invaded by a noxious smell coming from the nearby chemical plants. Neither the smell nor the air is quite as bad again—yet—as they were when I was a child, yet they are noticeably worse than they were just a year or two ago.

After such a short respite, thanks to the Clean Air Act, to smell again the poison air of youth constitutes a revolting Proustian moment. The odor dispels any thoughtlessly easy association of the passenger automobile, gasoline-powered, with freedom. It is not merely that the illusion of a painless recuperation of the melodies of youth is shattered by this industrial stink, but that the toxic smell induces a kind of psychic asphyxiation, a panicked sensation of being drawn back into a past from which we had hoped someday to emerge. The odor ultimately reminds me that as I race from here to there and back again I am complicit in the creation of loss, using up the planet, burning up petroleum, fossil memories, participating, like every driver, in a kind of global holocaust. And there it is, that terrible word, which I am usually so careful to avoid when speaking of the Nazi genocide.

This may seem a grandiose analogy. Such a grandiose analogy between two catastrophes, one hardly behind us and the other imminently before us, is by no means confined to a coterie of critical theorists on the left. In a 2004 book review in the *New York Times*, Phillip Bobbitt, a distinguished law professor at the

University of Texas, likens instead the weakness of Weimar to the lack of unity in a West putatively called to wage war on terrorism. Bobbitt writes:

> Weimar fell because too few enlightened liberals were willing to defend it, but I doubt this will be the case with the United States or with the West generally. Rather, it is another aspect of the Weimar experience, its internal lack of confidence, that 21st-century Western states will have to face up to. . . . It is not our enemies so much as our unpersuaded friends—as well as numbers of our fellow citizens—who will pose the most difficult challenges for leaders at war with terrorism.[7]

This is ominously jingoistic rhetoric indeed. Of course, it is not only the overly facile assumption that Weimar collapsed from weakness at its center that is troubling here. That is a debatable but defensible assertion. What is frightening, instead, is the open assertion that the greatest threat to American security comes from dissent within. Perhaps it can be understood as an unwise flourish to round off a hastily written review on a huge and complex subject, written by a decent and distinguished but overly busy scholar, for at the beginning of the review Bobbitt had written that in the case of the United States at least, "the complex of assumptions about Western culture" held by our "Occidentalist" enemies, whoever they may be, "are scarcely without foundation." Did Bobbitt, in suggesting American imperfections, mean to include himself among the "challenges for [our] leaders at war with terrorism?" Did he mean to include among those internal challenges Major General David H. Petraeus, commander of the 101st Airborne Division in Iraq, quoted elsewhere in that same edition of the *New York Times Book Review* as asking repeatedly the pointed question, "Tell me how this ends?"[8] Or the journalist Christopher Dickey, writing in that second review, "The wishful assumptions of the Pentagon civilians about the after-war were just as wildly off base as their intelligence about weapons of mass destruction?"

Of course not, and of course not, and of course not. But that does not remove the poisonous sting from rhetoric that identifies our own dissenting fellow citizens as worse than our enemies. I am almost afraid to talk about this, but I cannot escape the sense that Bobbitt's is the kind of rhetoric that you read, later, with astonishment that such a clear indication of a moment of danger could have been overlooked. You will thus excuse the intrusion of a more explicit politics, as I cannot exclude it although I do fear it, for it is so terrible to be wrong. There is no avoiding the recognition that our scholarship (now as in the 1930s) is inevitably shaped by our survival needs.

Triumphal oblivion becomes a waste we cannot afford. Citability of the past becomes not only a measure of redemption, but also a minimal condition for survival of the talking primate, of the species that speaks, of an anthropology of, and out of, Europe and its twentieth century.

You might wonder by now why I chose to dedicate this talk to the memory of Edward Said. It is not only because he was one of the most creative, passionate, and generous—if also one of the most combative—of the twentieth century's exiles. It is also because, even when speaking of things that happened long ago and far away, he was, both intellectually and emotionally, intensely *present*. Somehow missing him today reminds me of our own lost bard, Phil Ochs, who reminded us decades ago that knowing home and exile, knowing what's right and what's wrong, being able to sing about all this is actually only possible in the present, so we'd all better do it "while we're here."

5

Tropes of Home

I am writing on an airplane, somewhere over the Rockies.

I am speaking to you at the Kansas Union, not so high on the top of Mount Oread.

For more than a quarter-century, until just a couple of months ago, I was privileged to call "home," with a comforting lack of self-consciousness and an equally comforting sense of free choice, that place in America that, for its Jews at least, counts more than any other as a mythic place of origin. Now, suddenly, bracingly, confusingly, I no longer quite know where "home" is, and I suspect moreover that this is at least as much the norm in America as it is the exception. Tonight I want to share with you not a thesis and its defense about what "home" really means, in Jewish culture or in any other culture, but provisional results of my efforts to make fragments of sense out of what is still a very new and startling, if altogether welcome, turn in my life. The account must perforce be a picaresque one, even if it is not a classic tale of a quest, certainly not one with a find at its end.

I will start this brief, whirlwind journey in Jerusalem, the founding topos of home in Western civilization if ever there was one. But rather than the usual snapshot of the Western Wall in the foreground, the Dome of the Rock in the background, here is the home-page text for the Web site promoting the work of an artist who happens to work in the medium of decoupage. Now, I won't make too much of this, but it may be instructive that decoupage, as I understand it, involves taking an image and applying it to something seemingly more solid, almost the reverse of the rhetorical creation of "home," which rather involves taking something seemingly solid and applying it to an image. The Web site, then, for "Decoupage for the Soul" promotes the artwork of one Libi Astaire—a local girl, as she informs us:

> Decoupage for the Soul was founded in 2001 by Libi Astaire, an artist, writer and video director living in Jerusalem.
>
> Libi was born in Kansas City, Mo., grew up in Prairie Village, Kansas and spent most of her childhood trying to figure out why Dorothy preferred Kansas to Oz.
>
> That question started her on a search which led to studying theatre in London, poetry in New York and Chassidic thought in Jerusalem.
>
> For several years Libi was the manager of Colors of Jerusalem, an innovative Judaica art gallery located in the Jewish Quarter of Jerusalem's Old City. It was there that she began to see a way to successfully piece together her interests in art, poetry, Chassidic wisdom and the mysteries of the Hebrew language.
>
> The result is Decoupage for the Soul—a unique forum for Jewish thought and Jewish art.
>
> Now that she has found her way to Jerusalem, Libi is at last able to enthusiastically agree with Dorothy that "there's no place like home," and it is her hope that all Jews will find their way back home speedily and within our days.[1]

Let's spend a few seconds with this gem of the spidery World Wide Web. It appears that, like many Jewish families from this region, Libi's family migrated sometime in the later twentieth century, from the "old city"—that's Kansas City, Missouri, a place that plays no further role in Libi's story—to the other side, to the promised land of the suburbs of Johnson County, Kansas, to a "Prairie Village" that hardly looked like a village, that had no doubt already too many houses and too many trees to be taken for a prairie, that hardly looked like anything that could have been confused with the Kansas of Dorothy Gale; but perhaps Libi's parents were looking for better public schools, and let's hope they found them. Nevertheless, Libi's text elides her own "Prairie Village" with the black-and-white set of *The Wizard of Oz* and thus affords her a stark contrast between her asserted not-belonging in Kansas and Dorothy's iconic rootedness there. Less violently than a twister, I suppose, Libi's sense that she is not at home in Kansas sends her off on a quest at once aesthetic and Jewish, and it ends in an affirmation of personal wholeness, where she has successfully pieced together the various parts of her soul, where she can at last become—from a distance—the spiritual sister that, shall we say, Dorothy Gale never had until now, the one who understands the magic words of transport, which have borne Libi back to a home different from Dorothy's. Libi's concluding call to other Jewish souls both serves her commercial aims—*your* soul will be nourished by purchasing *my* artwork—and is, like so many calls from soul to soul, generous and imperious at once: Where I am, there shouldst, there may'st thou be also. And she doesn't mean a site on the Internet.

Libi Astaire isn't the only searcher, and I don't mean to make fun of or to exoticize her. My own *conscious* search for a home can best be said to have begun in late adolescence with a realization—unexpected but perhaps, if I may use the word, still overdetermined—that, to my distress, I wouldn't necessarily be at home anywhere in this America. As a college student, I arrived in Portland, Oregon, looked around the solid working-class neighborhood where my college was located, and said to myself, "My God, everybody here's *American*." A few months later I flew home for winter vacation, arrived at Newark Airport, and brought myself back down to earth, thinking, "That's silly, there are lots of different kinds of Americans, Jewish Americans, Italian Americans,

Black Americans. . . ." And then I returned to Portland, where I could not shake, once again, the powerful impression of "Americans" as a distinct ethnic group, one to which I did not belong.

Lower East Side

These peregrinations led me to settle, to graft myself as it were, onto New York City's Lower East Side; as I liked to say then, "After three generations, my family finally made it 'back' to the Lower East Side," although no ancestors, to my knowledge, had ever actually lived there. Still I knew, even before I got to this neighborhood where a number of synagogues, in buildings large and small, still kept the eternal light burning as congregations much too small for their buildings huddled around that lamp's dim warmth, that only when I found one where the smells and the accents felt like that old Farmingdale *shul* of my childhood—one, that, is, that felt like home—would I become a regular attendee. And I was rewarded with various moments of recognition, as if the neighborhood were saying to me, "Yes, young friend, this is where you belong":

- An elderly Satmar Hasid, still living on the Manhattan side though nearly all his comrades had moved to Brooklyn, noticed me wearing a yarmulke and reached out his hand in a wave that seemed to stretch all the way from his wheelchair to the sidewalk to caress me in welcome.
- When squatters in Tompkins Square Park "rioted" against the dispersal of their tent city, and municipal authorities railed against this anarchy, a senior historian recalled the protests, likewise called "riots," by immigrant Jewish housewives against the outrageous price of kosher meat in 1902.[2]
- At the same time, some even cast the neighborhood as a little

Palestine, dubbing the resistance to gentrification "Loisaida Intifada."

- It was even, almost, not too late to join or at least to walk in the footsteps of the Beat poets; inspired by one block on Norfolk Street, I dreamed of a book of poetry I would call *Dead Synagogue and Monument Factory*.

If I wrote that book today, I'd have to call it *Trendy Restaurant and Arts Center*. As it turns out, I wasn't the only young dreamer of a fantasized "return" to the Lower East Side, the place the ethnographic filmmaker Faye Lederman has dubbed "the new old country"; though my spouse Elissa Sampson and I were, in a sense, pioneers, and now find ourselves in at least one of these congregations *vatikim*, veteran resettlers, to borrow a term from the history of Zionism. In that congregation, founded by Anshe Brzezan, that is, Jews from the Galician town of Brzezan, no Brzezaner is left; the sheltering legal frame of the society Anshe Brzezan is now occupied by a younger generation, fictive and adopted Brzezaner all, making the synagogue their home wherever their ancestors may have come from.

And there on the Lower East Side we (really, it is Elissa's doing) have made a place that serves well the image of a home. Its guardians are a couple of cast metal lions, almost too big for our foyer, no doubt designed rather to serve as guardians of some fancy Westchester estate, that we have named Efayo and Shwartz. Their names, evoking a great New York toy store, echo Africa domesticated and Judaized. They are icons of a New York childhood, purchased in a moment of gross indulgence for our then-young son as consolation for the passing of his beloved Nanny, who would take him to the toy store, explaining that it was a museum where you could play with the toys, but not buy them. They are meant, and somehow do serve, to encapsulate a timespace I'll call "Jonah's New York," and indeed what they guard now is a shelf of books about the history of the Lower East Side and New York City generally.

History books, books of nostalgia, volumes of old photographs. The Lower East Side is a place people have desperately been trying to get away from for a long time; its Jewish population peaked by the early 1920s and has thus been enjoying a slow and elegiac decline for nearly a century. Although the Lower East Side is within walking distance of that fantasyland of Broadway, the first move, historically, at least for East European Jewish immigrants was yet farther away from Oz, to Williamsburg, Brooklyn, just across the river; to neighborhoods farther out, such as Brownsville, in that separate city turned borough; or, skipping midtown, to the Bronx or at least Harlem. As Julian Levinson has recently reminded us, Alfred Kazin's memoir *A Walker in the City* presents Brownsville as a kind of ghetto: "Beyond Brownsville was all 'the city,' that other land I could see for a day, but with every next day back on the block, back to the great wall behind the drugstore I relentlessly had to pound with a handball."[3] Nor was Kazin's evocation of beyond as "the city" at all idiosyncratic, as attested by the direction signs on some Brooklyn subway platforms that still, until just a few years ago at least, indicated trains going to Coney Island one way, trains headed "To City" going the other.

So Lower East Siders left for Brownsville, while dreamy Brownsville lads yearned for "the city." It is hard to imagine, in any case, that crowded residents of the Lower East Side had romantic fantasies of escaping to Brownsville, as likely a destination as that actually was. But at midcentury, the Lower East Side could still plausibly be imagined as a place from which the children of immigrant Jews might still dream of escaping. And indeed, we are informed, the choreographer Jerome Robbins's "original concept" of the show that eventually became *West Side Story* "was for a show titled East Side Story, treating . . . a love affair between an Italian-Catholic girl from Little Italy and an Orthodox Jewish boy from Mulberry Street and set at Easter-Passover time."[4]

Preserved despite the changes, from conception to execution, of ethnicities and neighborhoods, was the association of spaciousness with personal freedom for star-crossed lovers. And thus the emblematic song, titled with just one word, "Somewhere," a bridge—for me at least, trying as I am with your indulgence to construct for myself and for you this odd poetic bridge from one topos of "home" in America to the next—to the more poetically elaborated, if not more geographically precise, "Somewhere Over the Rainbow." It is not only the similar titles that suggest an elective affinity between the two songs. Both begin with two notes expressing, to my untrained ear, a similar interval, though musician colleagues inform me that the first interval is a full, confident octave, the latter perhaps a more tentative minor seventh. Certainly, though, both intervals soar upward, in a kind of musical representation of the singer's flying, as it were, toward a new home for the soul.

Kansas

Here we are then, flying as it were east to west, from Libi Astaire's Jerusalem, with a stopover in New York that for her is only an aesthetic place—the place where she studied theater—landing safely if with a bump or two and a thud, back in Kansas. I want to show you a film clip now, not from the movie you're expecting, but rather from *Splendor in the Grass*. The 1961 film turns, albeit not as centrally as *The Wizard of Oz*, on a hero's departure from Kansas—a departure here experienced not as liberating adventure, but as demoralizing exile, caused by his socially ambitious father's disastrous failure to recognize the hero's small-town, lower-class sweetheart as his *basherte*, his intended one. Here, well into the film's action, the character played by Warren Beatty and plainly enough named Bud pines in New Haven, where his father has sent him to acquire a four-year degree and corresponding worldly connections and class. Bud already knows that his heart's desire, in the form of Natalie Wood, is no farther than his own back yard. And Bud has no intention whatsoever of making his mark on the world, eventually finding himself drinking in an Italian place where the big-nosed waitress Angelina, soon to be his bride, worries that he's drinking too much and urges him to eat something—"a pizza":

DRUNKEN BUD: What is pizza?
ANGELINA: You don't know what pizza is? Where are you from?
BUD: From Kansas.
ANGELINA: Kansas—where is that?
BUD: It's right in the middle of the USA.
ANGELINA: So that's where your home is.
BUD: (Nods.)
ANGELINA: So what's it like out there in Kansas?

Bud is altogether mute when asked to describe Kansas, though he knows it well, other than to reinforce its bounded ordinariness, its very *middleness*, to coin an adjective. That blank image is not enough to satisfy the curiosity of the pioneer, and I am thus grateful that, while I was still contemplating Kansas as a destination rather than an origin, a learned colleague-to-be told me: "If you want to know Kansas history, read William Least Heat-Moon's *PrairyErth.*" I pass the kindness on, if kindness it will be for you as it was for me to suggest the reading of six hundred pages about Chase County—tallgrass prairie country with a human population of just three thousand. I don't think I've loved reading such a fat book quite so much since I was a child. It may be worthwhile considering *PrairyErth*, compendious as it is, as an instantiation of Walter Benjamin's description of the "full consciousness" of his imagined Messianic era, when "the past will be citable in all its moments." *PrairyErth* contains at any rate an intimation of what it would take, or what it once took, to make a home; so many things but, as in European Jewish diaspora communities, a cemetery perhaps first and foremost. Almost midway through this long mediation, Heat-Moon describes a walk through Prairie Grove cemetery, just outside of Cottonwood Falls. There he comes upon a marker reading, "MARGARET REPLOGLE SHORE 1921–1977. THANKS FOR STOPPING BY. SEE YOU LATER."[5] An eternal home indeed, a *beys oylem*, as we say in Yiddish.

In *PrairyErth*, Heat-Moon brings citations amply demonstrating that the trope of Kansas as the heartland, the essence, the "true home" of America long predate *The Wizard of Oz*. From a book by John James Ingalls, published in 1892, he quotes: "The statistics of the census tables are more eloquent than the tropes and phrases of the rhetorician. The story of Kansas needs no reinforcement from the imagination. Kansas is the navel of the nation."[6] So maybe I should have read to you from the census tables tonight. No, I don't think so; this quote from Ingalls is itself, of course, a highly rhetoricized statement, not least in its strikingly unmediated evocation of the body politic as a literal organism, not least in the catachrestic suggestion that this state, which in 1892 at least was certainly still much more a place immigrants came to than a place whose children left it, could be a place of origin: Kansas is figured here, it seems to me at least provisionally, as the source of the normative image of the American family.

Nor did the unlikely power of Kansas as a trope, a turning-toward in the American imagination, go unnoticed even a century ago, as Heat-Moon once again digests for us, this time from Carl Becker's book *Kansas* of 1910:

Kansas is no mere historical expression, but a "state of mind," a religion, and a philosophy in one.

The Kansas spirit is the American spirit double-distilled. It is a new-grafted product of American individualism, American idealism, American intolerance. Kansas is America in microcosm: as America conceives itself in respect to Europe, so Kansas conceives itself in respect to America.[7]

Microcosms are necessarily subject to selective representation, because there isn't room for everything in them. The Lower East Side is a navel or a microcosmic image of another, maybe an oddly complementary, America, and there is little room in that microcosm for memories of local violence, local protest such as the riots initiated by immigrant housewives in 1902 to protest against the outrageous price of kosher meat. Here in Kansas, too, we stand on a terrain of violence mostly forgotten in day-to-day life. Maybe it is the forgetting of violence that does, or can at least, constitute an image of home. Maybe the curious notion of Kansas as navel or microcosm for America, a "spirit double-distilled," came about as emblematic of the *national* effort to forget the violence of the Civil War decades. As Marilyn Robinson writes, in lines from her marvelous recent novel *Gilead* that would surely find their place in a new edition of *PrairyErth*, "people have forgotten. Remarkable things went on, certainly, but there has been so much trouble in the world since then it's hard to find time to think about Kansas."[8]

We should remember, then, that we are gathered on a hill by the site of a massacre, at the top of a burned and gentle town.

The story of Kansas as a frontier of Jewish dispersion, a story that some of you know more about than I ever hope to, much as I hope to learn about it, also is written in reminders of blood. As the official website of the American Jewish Historical Society relates the story,

In May 1856, [John] Brown led a raid on a company of Border Ruffians at Pottawatomie Creek and massacred more than a dozen of its members. The next day, Brown and his men captured 48 pro-slavery fighters at the Battle of Black Jack, a few miles from Palmyra.

August Bondi, Jacob Benjamin and Theodore Weiner all fought with Brown at Black Jack. In Bondi's account of the battle, which can be found in his papers at the American Jewish Historical Society, he recounts marching up a hill beside Brown, ahead of the other men:

> We walked with bent backs, nearly crawled, that the tall dead grass of the year before might somewhat hide us from the Border Ruffian marksmen, yet the bullets kept whistling. . . . Wiener puffed like a steamboat, hurrying behind me. I called out to him, "Nu, was meinen Sie jetzt" ("Now, what do you think of this?"). His answer, "Sof odom muves" (a Hebrew phrase meaning "the end of man is death," or in modern phraseology, "I guess we're up against it").[9]

"The end of man is death." As they say, more on that later. There is time remaining. What more can I say about Kansas, about the Lower East Side, about home?

More, at least, than the poor Bud, lost in New Haven, of *Splendor in the Grass*.

"There's No Place Like Home"

Bud's reply to Angelina's request that he locate Kansas for her is solipsistic, providing only information about the affect— ambivalent affect at that—the name bears for him: "Where's Kansas?" "It's where I live." There is thus a certain semantic equivalence between Bud's "It's where I live" and the magic words of power I've avoided uttering until now: "There's no place like home," which I should perhaps allude to as the quintagrammaton, TNPLH. Home can in a sense *only* be a trope, because in "There's no place like home," unless the speaker and the listener are from the same place there can logically be no intersubjective referent beyond the sense of displacement. The writer Salman Rushdie gets at something like this when he notes, "'There's no place like home' . . . is the least convincing idea in the film."[10] But he turns away from the potential insight into a real problematic of the notion of home, a complexity beyond sentimentalism, since he cannot resist adding a sardonic comment: "It's one thing for Dorothy to want to get home, quite another that she can only do so by eulogizing the ideal state which Kansas so obviously is not."[11] Rushdie, I should add, doesn't deny the *possibility* of home in the fashionable way that I am attempting or feigning to attempt. On the contrary, he adds in a further dig that we might most charitably read as anti-imperialist the claim to recall that when he first saw the film he "had a pretty good home, [while] Dorothy's place struck [him] as a dump."[12] In his commentary, Rushdie takes care at least to suggest that he is not "dumping" on *our* Kansas, since "If Oz is *nowhere*, then the studio setting of the Kansas scenes suggests that *so is Kansas*."[13]

In any case, none of this tells at all against the sentimental ending of *The Wizard of Oz*, since it is precisely the monochromatic plainness of Kansas that purports to mark that place as home. TNPLH is itself, of course, an allusion to the sampler staple, "Be it ever so humble, there's no place like home." And in an ideal American family—which Dorothy's adopted one cannot be—that lesson is to be learned from reading the writing on the wall, with no need to adventure beyond and discover, as Robert Cover wrote in a very different context and as the ancient Greek sophists, themselves foreigners and wanderers, also knew, that it is "the metaphor of separation [that] permits the allegory of dedication."[14] Indeed, the criticism made by Rushdie and by others, including some of my best new friends here in Kansas, that the ending of the movie version (unlike the book) of *The Wizard of*

Oz is profoundly reactionary, may be called into question by noting that, even in the movie, Dorothy has to recite the quintagrammaton as a magical incantation, to convince herself; it's not a statement containing a truth claim.

For all that, it's not an empty or a meaningless statement, any more than casting Kansas as microcosm is merely the promotion of false consciousness. Our minds, like our culture, work tropically. As the psychologist Wilfred Ruprecht Bion points out, not only collective rhetoric, but also "more general psychic operations . . . involve incessant breaking into parts and building into wholes."[15] (In that perspective, and particularly in the decades after the War Between the States, it's hardly surprising that a *state*, Kansas, would be taken as a metonymy of America.)

What the quintagrammaton TNPLH does—perhaps like bloody Kansas recast by John James Ingalls as the fictive, bodily birthplace of all Americans, those, that is, on either side of the color line, on either side of the Mason-Dixon line—is create an aura of empathy, only not by evoking the same image but rather the same feeling. We don't have to have the same home to be Americans. "There's no place like home" is really meant to evoke a different place in different hearers.

Telz

Or a different sound. "Dorothy! Dorothy!" "I cash clothes!" For me, a sound that might evoke something like home is a sentence that my mother, Alice, who is here this evening, passed on orally. She heard it from her father, who heard it, as a young boy, in the Lithuanian yeshiva town of Telz—Telshiai in Lithuanian—from an elderly teacher. That young boy and that elderly teacher stood together, watching youngsters play, and the elderly teacher wistfully allowed a doubt about the strictness with which he himself had been raised: "*Un vos volt geven shlekht, eybe mir hobn a shprung geton?*" (What harm would it have done if we lads had been allowed to play a bit?)

Elissa and I visited Telz this spring, and we were rewarded with the sight of the old—really quite modest—yeshiva building, falling shards of whose bricks we brought back with us like relics, and with a visit to the intact grave of my mother's father's mother. I allowed myself briefly to fantasize reestablishing the Telz yeshiva (whose heritage is carried on, not in Kansas but in Cleveland)—of reestablishing it, that is, in this Lithuanian city of Telshiai. Or at least, of coming back, entering the abandoned yeshiva building, and spending a bit of time studying Torah there.

I don't mean to suggest for a minute—well, I do mean to suggest, but certainly not for more than a minute—that doing so would mean, in a psychic sense or in some more cosmic sense, a retrieval of "home." The suggestion isn't just that you can't go home again; the suggestion is that, if your heart's desire isn't there, you never really lost it to begin with. How would you know when you've *really* gotten back home?

That you'll never know it in this world is the hard and mournful conclusion slyly wrapped in a seeming tearjerker country song that was big a couple of years back, Craig Morgan's "Almost Home." The narrator relates seeing an old homeless man close to death, "curled up behind some garbage cans" on a bitter cold night, wakes him, and is told that in the old man's dream, he was "almost home."

Is this the last word, that the only true meaning of home anymore is death? Remember that when Angelina said, "So that's where your home is," Bud could only nod silent assent. What, I wonder, did Warren Beatty suppose his character's "motivation" to be at that moment? What does his silence suppress? A melodramatic awareness that he suddenly no longer knows where home is, after all? The urge to burst out weeping, as he senses that his desperate loneliness has somehow been sensed? Sheer mortification at coming from a place where they *don't even know what pizza is?*

Bud isn't the only one who has a hard time talking about home; in a way, his muteness was prescient. Rushdie mourns: "'Home' has become a scattered, damaged, hydra-various concept in our present travails. There is so much to yearn for. There are so few rainbows anymore."[16]

Have we, irretrievably, lost our way home? But I have seen a rainbow, right here, in Kansas, on my way to the Louisburg cider mill.

6

A Moment of Danger, a Taste of Death

Meir Katz kindly asked me to write an article for a special issue of the *Cardozo Law Review* devoted to Walter Benjamin and the law. I decided to take the opportunity to resume my attempt, fruitless so far, to articulate the difficulty we have of imagining the future with composure and with any sense of competent responsibility. The difficulty for me of such thinking has long been linked to Benjamin's image of the Angel of History resolutely turned against the future: I keep wishing to shout, in a street voice, "Yo, Angel! Turn around!" But I do not find that voice. Seeking some other who has tried to think with and beyond Benjamin on the future, I found, first, Owen Ware's article "Dialectic of the Past / Disjuncture of the Future: Derrida and Benjamin on the Concept of Messianism"[1] and, through it, Jacques Derrida's *Specters of Marx*.[2] Then, one Sunday early in September 2004, as I worked through Derrida's book, I had a richly relevant email exchange with my college friend Martin Land, a theoretical physicist now living in Jerusalem. This very tentative contribution, then, begins with that day's correspondence. It continues with my notes and commentary on the general problem of imagining the future without the support of a notion of progress, and ends with Martin Land's afterthoughts and response to my notes and commentary.

MARTIN: I checked out some of the names we've been throwing around on the Reed alumni directory. JG is a partner at some big law firm. The only Reed physics graduate I ever hear about is Barbara Ehrenreich.

JONATHAN: Yeah, I came across JG's name when I was in the middle of my disastrous search for a second law firm job. They couldn't interview me because they had a client conflict with my previous firm. JG could have been my boss. I imagine her in court with long, straight brown hair, an army shirt, and jeans, but that's probably inaccurate.

MARTIN: Yes, probably inaccurate. It sounds like you're describing my brother. I don't think that he goes into court that way, but he might as well. He is also retiring from the practice of law, under circumstances slightly different than yours but for the same basic reason. He claims that after he got stiffed by all the rich kids he sprung during the World Trade Organization demonstrations, he has no interest in volunteering for the National Lawyers Guild during the Republican convention. I wonder what his excuse will be this time for spending thirty-six consecutive hours in court pro bono. Maybe he should just admit that he was born a social worker, not a lawyer.

JONATHAN: I wish those demonstrators wouldn't. It's not going to help us get rid of Bush, and that is the only, only, only thing I care about now. I am afraid. It feels like we're playing chicken with history.

MARTIN: Oh, pshaw! Next you're going to say that the Serbian nationalists shouldn't have assassinated the Archduke Ferdinand.

It's like in *Rebel Without a Cause*—right before they played an actual game of chicken, James Dean says to the other guy, "Why do we do this?" and the other guy answers, "You gotta do something." I am less concerned by what people will do than by what they are not doing. You're right that not much will be accomplished at this point by simply registering a protest, peaceful or otherwise. But the problem is that, as Trotsky essentially described the descent into fascism in Europe, the middle class in the United States (or in that old-fashioned language, the masses of the proletariat) is convinced that it has more to fear from "chaos" than from repression. As Benjamin Franklin said, "They that would give up essential liberty to obtain a little temporary safety deserve neither liberty nor safety." Just once, I would like to see a U.S. president impeached for lying, corruption, repression, and warmongering, instead of for getting a blowjob.

JONATHAN: I agree, as long as it's Kerry rather than Bush. The Republicans have announced that they're going to claim that the Democrats are behind the protests. They will do so successfully. People will buy it. Bush will be reelected, and he will not be impeached for any reason.

MARTIN: I see no reason to dispute your concerns. But you do agree that you are saying, in slightly more diplomatic language, that the American people are about a month behind where the German people were when Hitler succeeded in convincing them that the communists had burned down the Reichstag. If so, then I don't see any reason for optimism of any kind in any direction, and would go so far as to say that planning for a year from now seems slightly delusional.

JONATHAN: Well, there you are. It's not obvious what one is supposed to do in a hopeless situation. But self-righteous self-expression that is destined to ensure disaster seems unwise. Hey, I can't stop these people, can I? I'm just saying that I think it's very unwise. I can't help thinking that Lenin would agree.

MARTIN: When the situation in Russia was less than supportive of his ideas, he took off for London and didn't come back until things had changed. But that was in the days when intraplanetary distances had the likelihood of protecting the lucky from calamity. Unless you know a way to get off this rock, I think it's time to bend over and kiss your ass goodbye.

Meanwhile, Bush's leak about "a covert shift in policy toward the settlements" has been received in Israel as a huge success for the people opposing Sharon from the right. The pundits are all saying that by applying pressure to Sharon, the settlers have extracted an unprecedented concession from the United States. Now what?

JONATHAN: This weekend is the second annual Lower East Side "Howl!" Festival, in the midst of which Elissa is doing a couple of East Village synagogue tours. So we were watching a video clip of an interview with Allen Ginsberg, shot in his apartment around the corner from here. He mentions that he'd taken a nap, and during the nap he dreamed he was talking to his friend Carl Solomon, who was dead.

"So I asked him, 'What's it like being dead?' He told me, 'Well, it's really like the [mental] hospital. You get along okay if you play by the rules.' So I asked him, 'What are the rules?' He told me, 'There are two rules. One, you have to remember you're dead. And two, you have to act like you're dead.'"

MARTIN: Interesting dream. Of course, you could say the same about being alive. There's a popular song here (well, it's not very popular) called, "It's no big deal, this 'World to Come.'" The verses are like, "It's no big deal, this 'World to Come,'" "things don't work very well here either," "there's a government here too," "there are rich and poor in heaven too," and so on. Death seems to be a popular metaphor for life, now that I think about it. I guess it's like Kafka said, "The meaning of life is that it ends."

JONATHAN: In either case (whether you're remembering to act like you're alive or remembering to act like you're dead) there's a refreshing reminder of contingency. I'm trying to escape my worries by making a great big pot of vegetable soup for yontev. And by reading Derrida's *Specters of Marx* (that's not to escape my worries, that's to help me write my paper about what to do about the fact that Walter Benjamin does not help us to think about the future, he only destroys in us the illusion of progress). He's brilliant and eloquent but so verbose and it's all probably pretty useless. The only thing he seems to be saying is, just because your past vision of a future Redemption obviously isn't going to turn out the way you thought it was when you were young doesn't mean you can give up being responsible toward the Other who is to come. Which is roughly equivalent, in the present crisis, to the saying of some Hasidic rebbe or other that despair is the greatest sin.

MARTIN: My thesis advisor had a calligraphed poster on his wall that said, "We haven't seen everything yet, but when we do, it won't be the first time." In the formulation of physics that we work in, there are two separate quantities called time, and each is represented by a different symbol. The coordinate time (or the Einstein time, represented by the letter t) is what our watch reads, and it's a coordinate in the same sense as a map coordinate—a place. The historical time (or invariant time, represented by the Greek letter tau) is a parameter (a number) that just keeps getting uniformly bigger all the time, so it can be used to keep track of what happens before or after other things. In the ordinary experience of people with little imagination, the two times seem to be the same, but after giving it a little thought, it becomes pretty clear that as the historical time tau goes on, the coordinate time t can sometimes get bigger, sometimes it seems to slow down, and sometimes it can even go backward. But it also has implications for how we understand our "progress" and our memories. By this theory, there may be multiple occurrences of the events that were recorded when the coordinate time read October 25, 1917 (including those when the historical time also read that time), but the events that are relevant to us now are the ones recorded when the coordinate time reads October 25, 1917, and the historical time reads August 22, 2004. Same place, but maybe not the same events. You could even go back to visit Paris in 1939, but it would still be the Paris 1939 of now, not the one of then. Who knows what you'd find. That's why the trick for scholars is to know the difference between the then of then and the then of now— both are equally real, but they may not be of equal importance (importance in the conventional sense of influence and consequence). This is, among other things, a physics that allows for actual change—the awfulness of some childhood event may still be with me, but only as the then of now, because the then of then stayed right where it happened. The then of now doesn't have to influence me in the same way that the then of then did. It works for the future too. The future that gets here is never the future we have when we anticipate it, even if both are equally real. Now if that seemed less convoluted than Derrida, I may actually succeed in explaining it some day.

Are you cooking for rosh hashona already, or is there some yontif that I've overlooked?

JONATHAN: Does that mean that, even though my best rational analysis of "the way things are going" leaves little room to doubt the inevitability of extinction in the fairly near term, it may not be reasonable to despair now? Also, since this is a difficult paper for me, do you have any thoughts on the role of language in structuring / determining these times? I am especially interested in structuring / responsibility toward the future; my paper is called "Law, Language and the Subject of the Future," and my fullest task, which I cannot succeed at, is to elucidate the liberal assumptions about the "subject" as subject to law in a way that helps us understand how little able we have been to structure law (lawlike behavior, behavior that sustains the subject's representation of itself as a lawful subject worthy of a future) in a way that is responsible toward the future. If all we can say is that the future-then (the "future to come," in something more like Derrida's words) will not be like the future-now (the "future-present," in Derrida's term), how does that help us act toward the future now? I'm cooking for the rosh hashona of now. And believe me, I have a freezer. (This, let me remind you explicitly, is a paraphrase of R. Crumb: "This is a story of a man who went looking for America. And believe me, he took along a lunch.")

P.S. Before, when I wanted to send you the Allen Ginsberg anecdote, I went to the "G"s in my e-mail address book. Now, when I want to send you this quote from Derrida, I went to the "D"s.

JONATHAN: Referring (in the course of an enjoyable skewering of Fukuyama) to the expectation as late as the early 1980s that the Eastern European dictatorships might remain for a long, long time, Derrida writes of the need not to rely "on the simple (ideal, mechanical or dialectical) opposition of the real presence of the real present or the living present to its ghostly simulacrum, the opposition of the effective or actual (*wirklich*) to the non-effective, inactual, which is also to say, as long as one relies on a general temporality or an historical temporality made up of the *successive* linking of presents identical to themselves and contemporary with themselves."[3]

   I find this quite lucid and presume it is consistent with your thinking about time(s).

MARTIN: Wow, that quote from Derrida is remarkably close to what I was writing when it arrived: Well, there is the future that exists now, and it is the only future that we can discuss now. But it may not happen. On the other hand, there is an important distinction between despairing of the future that we can "see" and despairing because we have a fairly accurate sense of the actual conditions now that will affect whatever future emerges. The first despair is fairly baseless, but the second is pretty well founded (within our ability to make predictions about the outcomes of very complex systems that have a habit of behaving dialectically and nonlinearly).

   A better reason for despair is what is happening right now, because there's not much controversy over what's going on (there are people who think it's good, but the ones who deny what's going on now are part of the good reason for despair and there is no reason to allow their opinions to influence ours), and because it's bad now.

JONATHAN: I don't despair about the present, heartless as that may seem. We have already lived through the worst that we could possibly survive to witness and remember. What terrifies me is the prospect of an extinction so total that memory itself, language, would disappear as well—that this event of consciousness per se would have reached its finite point.

MARTIN: What I meant when I said that it's really bad now is not that the level of suffering is comparable with those within recent memory. I meant that based on our understanding of human affairs, we have strong reason to predict that from where we are now, extinction is a strong possibility. But, if this isn't too academic a distinction when we're talking about extinction, my despair is for those causes in the present, not for the possible extinction in the future. Someone wants to make me extinct? They'll be doing me a favor. On the other hand, the despair of the present is here now, and sometimes I kick myself for having kids.

JONATHAN: Yeah, but you did have kids. So did I. Moreover, we're hardly the first generation that thought it was crazy to have done so. Which doesn't mean that, just as we are their grandchildren, so there will be a world for their grandchildren as well. Which also (again) is why I'm struggling with the inadequacy of Benjamin's notion that what fuels messianic (or revolutionary) longing is the image of "enslaved ancestors" rather than "liberated grandchildren." Liberated, hah! How about surviving?

MARTIN: Maybe Benjamin wasn't praising the fuel for messianic longing as much as he was describing it. Living in the

Middle East, it seems to me entirely commonplace that people are more motivated to avenge an ancient slight than to either "liberate" the future for their grandchildren or make the world a better place in the present. People hold weddings and bar mitzvahs on Masada, the site of ancient tragedy. There is no similar celebration of the heroism of Yohanan ben Zakai, who got down on his knees before the Roman governor and pleaded to allow the continuation of Jewish study, even though the State of Israel owes its existence to him, more than to Masada. In a sense, in choosing to serve the needs of the past or those of the future, we're indicating not only what we see as important, but also what we understand to be real. I understand the book of Deuteronomy to be saying that the Law is a blueprint for a just society. *Lo b'shamaim he* (the Law is in the physical world, not in Heaven). You follow the Law, things right here will be relatively well organized and that's good. When you don't follow the Law, things will be all messed up, right here and now, and the immediate material consequences are the only "punishment" you need. But when the locus of attention shifts to the "other" world (where otherness may mean the past, the supernatural, or the purely subjective) we approach the slippery slope of human spiritual need. Yeshayahu Leibowitz was troubled about our tendency to confuse our needs with God's will, and thereby falsely attribute holiness to desires arising from purely human concerns (weaknesses). Once we start down that slope, we're on the road to the Jim Jones Kool-Aid stand.

Another idea that has been occupying me for the last year is related to the ideas of law and of time. I have become increasingly convinced of the importance of examining the academic assumption (or conceit) that most (or even many) people hold ideas or even opinions. Where is the evidence that most individuals expect of themselves that they must maintain a consistent (both in the sense of consistent over time and in the sense of not self-contradictory) body of statements that they understand to be well grounded or to which they remain loyal? And how do we investigate this question, given that a big part of being "western" is to be able to act as though one does?

When the *New York Post* celebrates the denial of airline service to a U.S. Senator as "it sounds like airport screeners are finally getting their act together. . . . Isn't that the way toughened airline security is supposed to work?" does this convince you that there is any actual "holding of opinions" going on here, so much as there is "writing of words"— words that can be written one moment and disregarded the next moment? When people want lower taxes and more government services, should we dignify these impossibly inconsistent desires by calling them opinions? Aside from the standard anthropological explanations of social reciprocity and fixing of group boundaries, why do intellectuals keep acting as though the "average guy" shares their fascination with the formulation, cataloging, and maintenance of correct statements? Try to bring that attitude to the Middle East and see how far it gets you. In all seriousness and with as little denigration as I am capable of, I claim that one of the main "frictions" in this part of the world is between those who take for granted this "western" expectation that we are supposed to have our mental catalogs in order and are embarrassed by those who don't, and those who take for granted that there is a "traditional" off-the-shelf formulation available for every occasion, which requires no consistency check against either "empirical reality" or anything else that one has ever said, with this latter group not having any idea what the former group wants from their lives.

On Friday morning, there was a minor car accident in

front of my house, with (*baruch Hash-m*) injuries only to a pair of male egos. Now some might think that automobile traffic is an area in which the applicability of written law is not controversial, but those people have not lived among the Jews of Jerusalem. One car made a left turn onto a one-way street, so it should have been a fairly simple question of right of way (the driver who turned did not yield as required by law). This, not to mention that we have no-fault insurance, and it made absolutely no pecuniary difference to anyone who was responsible. Well, that had nothing to do with the ensuing screaming and yelling for either side. Both drivers began with the approach that "I wanted to go, so you should have stopped." Then, there was a recital of the encyclopedia of Israeli slogans, from "Nothing like this ever happened before!" to remarks about female siblings and their genitalia.

So if you ask me why we have not been able to implement liberal assumptions about law into a structure that is responsible toward the future, the answer is that liberal assumptions about lawfulness have not been internalized, even by the bourgeoisie for whom liberalism and lawfulness are necessary parts of the technology of capitalism. The difference between Democrats and Republicans is just this question. The Democrats want to bequeath power to their own offspring, so they seek law to stabilize the system, while the Republicans believe in the short-term efficacy of force and "*après moi, le deluge.*" Most people never give it a moment's thought. The only people who agonize about it all are the intellectuals, who have nothing to sell but our scribbling.

Jonathan's Notes and Commentaries

It may be useful to try to identify some of the barriers to our thinking, imagining, or discussing possible futures in ways that are as responsible to them as we need to be, always now:

1. *The shock of postmodernity*, still with us in the sense that we still hardly know what to do/what to want now that the "modern" is only a memory of a promised "future" that, to our bewilderment, lies behind us. Brian Massumi identifies the temporal place of what I term this "loss of the future" (in America) with the assassination of President Kennedy—which does seem to me to have resonance.

> The assassination of John F. Kennedy marks a divide in American culture. . . . No longer was it possible for Americans to have a sense of oneness stretching back in time to a golden age waiting just over the next horizon for the long-expected return of the citizens of progress. . . . Diachrony would never be the same.[4]

2. *Regret at our collective failure*—a failure represented by the concatenation of disappointed revolutions and by the ultimate impossibility of assimilating the military defeat of fascism to any credible narrative of universal progress. And maybe this regret is in fact easier than facing forward:

> There's a generally accepted rule that repentance consists of two aspects: first, regretting one's past sins; and second, committing oneself to act decently from now on. It's psychologically easier to become suffused with a sense of regret and think about the ugly past, than to become suffused by a vision of commitment and think about a beautiful future.[5]

Of course, suggesting that we read history as *our own* failure implies a collective responsibility for history on the part of the human species, rather than a bifurcation into good ("progressive") and bad ("reactionary") camps—an issue on which Benjamin's Theses are themselves ambivalent.

3. *Despair*, which is not merely the absence of hope. I propose instead two ways of thinking about despair of the future. First, it is a product of our ingrained tendency to assume that if we do not hope then disaster is inevitable. It is axiomatic for me (though perhaps this is just some fond Benjaminian orthodoxy) that any possibility of turning the Angel to face the future must be accomplished without the use of "hope." Second, paradoxical though it may seem, despair reflects our inexperience at articulating the possibility of annihilation (would the Angel be even more discouraged to face forward and see a pile of rubble growing ever larger receding into an unmarked future?). This possibility Derrida acknowledges unambiguously: "To fail in everything, it is true, will always remain possible. Nothing will ever give us any insurance against this risk, still less against this feeling."[6]

4. *The association of future-talk with capitalist consumerism*, which might be rethought as resistance to the operationalization of time, for instance, in calculations of the "time value of money," related to capitalist consumerism, as Massumi describes with terrifying lucidity:

> The accident as advent and threat: the pure past of the sudden and uncontrollable contingency, and the uncertain future of its recurrence. Future-past. The hinge-commodity, in its double modality of consummation/consumption, fills the hyphenated gap between past and future, holding the place of the present (Lynn *is wearing* a dress watch . . . it *has* a secure buckle . . . it *costs* . . .). Buying *is* (our present/presence). The commodity is a time-buckle, and the time-buckle is a safety belt. The consumer "good" reassures us that we are, and traditionally, will continue to be, unfallen from our groundless peak. Buying is prevention. It insures against death.
>
> The inevitable. We all know our time will come. But if we follow the existential imperative of capitalism—don't crack

under pressure (pick the right watch)—we don't have to worry about never having been. Even if we take a licking, our consumer heritage will keep on ticking. We will live on in the sparkle of our great-great-grandchildren's fashion accessories.[7]

To which my brother Daniel, expecting soon the arrival of his own first grandchild, responds: "*halevay!*"—would that we could so believe in our great-great-grandchildren's sparkling lives!

5. *A misplaced guarantee of freedom for our descendants*:

> We have no right to look upon future citizens as if we were master gardeners. . . . (Hence, a) system of liberal education provides children with a sense of the very different lives that could be theirs—so that, as they approach maturity, they have the cultural materials available to build lives equal to their evolving conceptions of the good.[8]

This impulse to leave the future "open" for our descendants might help explain in turn the poverty, if not total absence, or our legal language for responsibility to the future.[9]

6. Finally, and at any rate for me, *Benjamin's own injunction*, which he casts as a prohibition observed by "the Jews," against "investigating the future."[10]

Does the Angel of History, then, *forbid* us from contemplating the future? How could we, "breeders," possibly observe such an inhuman demand? How could we not worry about our grandchildren? Is there something debilitating about the urgency of Benjamin's refusal of complacency, of normalcy, of progress? *Within* recognition that "the state of emergency is not the exception but the rule," is there a place, for example, for Judith Butler's notion of iteration?[11] Is "iteration" necessarily gradualist? Or, from another angle, how wedded should we be to Benjamin's desperate formulation of the supposed *strategic* mistake of the European left in the 1930s, especially given the entirely plausible claim (startling at first to those of us schooled, for example, on the importance of Benjamin's critique of the Social Democrats, but nevertheless compelling as soon as it is articulated) that by the 1930s it was too late for intellectual or artistic opposition to stop the domination of European fascism?[12]

Owen Ware, weighing Benjamin's messianic articulation against Derrida's, does find it lacking: "To his own detriment, Benjamin is incapable of conceiving of any futurity outside the notion of progress, and for this reason alone, he is incapable of approaching any concept of the future-to-come."[13] The reference to Benjamin's "detriment" sounds a sour and uncharitable note, not only because Benjamin, too, clearly did at least attempt to refuse to surrender to a future of "empty, homogeneous time,"[14] but because of the implausible suggestion that Benjamin's own situation might somehow have been better had he been more lucid, or perhaps more "hopeful." How? By really making it possible for him, instead of dying at Port-Bou, to be "cart[ed] . . . up and down the [United States] as the last European"?[15] Likewise, it seems wrong to speak of a "concern for the future simply lacking in Benjamin's understanding of a messianism devoted to the past."[16] This "lack" in the Theses is anything but simple; neither can it be correct to describe Benjamin's desperation as a lack of concern. Ware's supposition that there *is* no future in Benjamin's vision perhaps also explains his misleading assertion that, for Benjamin, "We are not 'enslaved ancestors' but 'liberated grandchildren;'"[17] Thesis XII is not an assertion about who "we," the generation of any present, is, but about the "image" (ascendant rather than descendant) that nourishes revolutionary passion.[18]

While Ware acknowledges that both Benjamin and Derrida re-
sisted "the model of objective, linear time,"[19] it seems to me that
he himself reverts to such a conventionalized notion—and im-
putes it both to Benjamin and to "traditional" messianism—by
describing "Benjamin's understanding of messianic time as in-
verted Messianism."[20] Ware elaborates on this formulation: "The
great reversal accomplished with Benjamin's weak messianism is
not the Marxist appropriation of a theological term, but the inver-
sion of a messianic gaze, traditionally directed to the future, but
now to the past instead."[21] After decades of debate about the relation between Benjamin's "Theses" and "Jewish Messianism," I
think it can safely be said that, against a progressive eradication
of the past, he invoked a "traditional" rhetoric of redemptive longing that was, in Gershom Scholem's words, both "restorative and
utopian"[22] and that, perhaps also, was unencumbered by a secularized, linear notion of progress[23] so that it could readily exist in
a time out of joint, waiting but not patiently for one who "comes
suddenly, unannounced, and precisely when he is least expected
or when hope has long been abandoned."[24]

Nevertheless, Ware's critique of Benjamin is on point in a fundamental way. "Simple" or not, there *is* a lack in Benjamin's formulation that must torment us, living after the catastrophe that
tumbled over the back of his Angel and facing, willy-nilly, another
and more final one. We have a need, even if one that cannot be
met, to think how we can think in some way commensurate with
the possibility of the future. And here Benjamin does not seem to
help us.

Seeking, presumably, to address that lack, Ware proposes that
Derrida's is a more "promising" (so to speak) articulation of a
stance vis-à-vis time and messianic possibility than Benjamin's:

> I hold that Benjamin's model of weak messianism is incapable of
> approaching the messianic promise to-come [a phrase based on

Derrida's *"l'a-venir"*]. . . . In order to account for the heterogeneity of the messianic, Derrida recasts time as out-of-joint, thereby viewing the future not as a future-present, but as a heterogeneous *other.* The possible influence this new conception of time has on our understanding of the subject, however, remains an open question.[25]

Derrida seems to concur that his messianic "logic" supplements Benjamin's by being future-oriented:

> Let us quote [the Theses] for what is consonant there, despite many differences and keeping relative proportions in mind, with what we are trying to say here about a certain messianic destitution, in a spectral logic of inheritance and generations, *but a logic turned toward the future no less than the past, in a heterogeneous and disjointed time.*[26]

Yet Derrida does not seem to me so much to be proposing a "new conception of time," as Ware suggests (partly, but not only, because the notion of novelty must be undermined in a disjointed time), but rather doing a kind of redemptive or restorative work (*Specters of Marx* itself being, above all, an invocation of the necessity of Marx written just as the "short twentieth century"[27] was ending). Benjamin's final Thesis telescopes the notion of a future *not* arrived at "progressively" into something waiting beyond a narrow "gate,"[28] and thus leaves us at risk, as overly loyal readers, of refusing even the very *problem* of contemplating the future. Derrida reaffirms and elaborates, for us (and here is what I take as the core of Ware's aperçu), the contours of something like a stance of nonlinear expectation, even stripped of what Ware calls "teleo-eschatological"[29] content:

> By affirming the impossibility of a teleo-eschatological self, the messianic subject, by contrast, affirms the promise of the unforeseeable future-to-come: "The self, the *autos* of legitimating and legitimated self-foundation, *is still to* come, not as a future reality but as that which will always retain the essential structure of a promise and as that which can only arrive as such, as *to come.*"[30]

Derrida's text wonders both about the status of the "promise" (are we the promissors or those to whom the promise is made?) and about who "we" are (children of Abraham or everyone?). On one hand, Derrida seems to suggest that we are the ones who "promise:" "the pledge or the promise (the oath, if one prefers: 'swear!'), the originary performativity that does not conform to preexisting conventions." It seems it could not be God who would be described as not conforming here, that this preexisting command to swear not conventionally but *now*, is addressed to humans, in their contingent time. And yet, Derrida also suggests that a "promise" toward the future is what any law worthy of the name, presumably including but not limited to a divine law, carries within itself:

> Apparently "formalist," this [here, Kojève's] indifference to the content has perhaps the value of giving one to think the necessarily pure and purely necessary form of the future as such, in its being-necessarily-promised, prescribed, assigned, enjoined, in the necessarily formal necessity of its possibility—in short, in its law. It is this law that dislodges any present out of its contemporaneity with itself. Whether the present promises this or that, whether it be fulfilled or not, or whether it be unfulfillable, there is necessarily some promise and therefore some historicity as future-to-come. It is what we are nicknaming the messianic without messianism.[31]

Perhaps what this adds to Benjamin's formulation is indeed the notion of a possible constellation, or "contemporaneity" between the present and—not itself, and not only some moment in the past—but a moment in some as yet unimagined future.[32] And yet it still echoes, in its urgency, something as old as the increased importance for Jews, in the context of Jewish-Christian disputations in the later Middle Ages, of the insistence that the Messiah is indeed *to come*: "Jews devoid of conviction in eventual redemption would have been helpless in the face of the Christian onslaught. Jews had to continue to believe and their leaders had to foster that belief."[33] Derrida recasts this by reducing it to the imperative: "Not only must one not renounce the emancipatory desire, it is necessary to insist on it more than ever, it seems, and insist on it, moreover, as the very indestructibility of the 'it is necessary.'"[34] The need to resist *moral* defeat is still present. This is not, yet, the language of the Angel of History staring unblinkered into the future.

The question, in turn, of whom the messianic promise "covers"—to whom it is made, or whom it obligates, Derrida leaves teasingly, achingly open:

> Many young people today . . . probably no longer sufficiently realize it: the eschatological themes of the 'end of history,' of the 'end of Marxism,' of the 'end of philosophy,' of the 'ends of man,' of the 'last man' and so forth were, in the '50s, that is, forty years ago, our daily bread. We had this bread of apocalypse in our mouths naturally, already, just as naturally as that which I nicknamed after the fact, in 1980, the 'apocalyptic tone in philosophy.'
>
> What was its consistency? What did it taste like?[35]

The biblical allusions to a term of forty years and to "daily bread," with the added questions about the character of this bread, suggest that Derrida is thinking of manna for the generation in the desert, already placing into question how purely Derrida wished to propose a promise fully without content. But perhaps this bread of apocalypse recalls as well the wafer of communion.

Associating manna with the Eucharist would in any case be consistent with Derrida's question "how to relate, but also how to dissociate the two messianic spaces we are talking about here under the same name? If the messianic appeal belongs properly to a universal structure . . . how is one to *think* it *with* the figures of Abrahamic messianism?"[36] A question Derrida answers by evoking, unmistakably to my ears at least, Abraham waiting at the opening of his tent at the heat of the day (for visitors, it must be

added for the sake of an ever-renewed openness, who will announce the coming of a son):

> Without . . . despair and if one could *count* on what is coming, hope
> would be but the calculation of a program. One would have the pros-
> pect but one would not longer wait for anything or anyone. Law with-
> out justice. One would no longer invite, either body or soul, no longer
> receive any visits, no longer even think to see. To see coming. Some,
> and I do not exclude myself, will find this despairing 'messianism' has
> a curious taste, a taste of death. It is true that this taste is above all a
> taste, a foretaste, and in essence it is curious. Curious of the very thing
> that it conjures—and that leaves something to be desired.[37]

Hope without despair is forbidden; redemption has the taste of
death. Something to be desired, of course: What could it possibly
mean, really, to know how to talk about the future?

Response from Martin Land

To the extent that postmodernism represents the most advanced
thinking of our time (sidestepping the implied teleology in the
word *advanced*), the theoretical physicist is triply out of date, en-
gaging in a craft that not only predates modernism, but that has
been practiced, with essentially unchanged assumptions, long
enough to have served as inspiration for modernism's anteced-
ents in the Enlightenment. Fortunately for physics, people are still
concerned, despite differences in emphasis, with the questions
that occupied Galileo and Newton—relationship, change, and
causality—and continue to recognize analysis/deconstruction as
a legitimate pastime for curious minds. Unfortunately for other
varieties of discourse, admiration of the language of science has
often had a stifling effect, and with particular relevance to the
present discussion, prescientific ideas about time—a useful vo-
cabulary in discussing the moment between past and future—

have been denigrated in the name of progress, despite the abandonment by physics of the popular contemporary conception of absolute linear time, over a century ago. Worse yet, the success of science on its own terms, as a path to a certain kind of insight based on limiting the field of study to phenomena that can be manipulated and repeated, is often taken to deny the legitimate consideration of phenomena outside the realm of the controllable. So, while wary at seeming to announce the lessons of science as necessary truths for ready application to all questions, it was natural for me to offer certain constructs from contemporary physics to Jonathan Boyarin as potentially suggestive metaphors for thinking about the future. This ongoing collaboration, now separated by ten thousand miles and thirty years from its starting point, remains remarkably similar in tone to its college-pub roots (especially the ancient personal peeves). We have been imagining the future together for long enough that much of that future is now long in the past. It is not obvious that observing these changes in chronological categorization has had much effect on our underlying concerns.

The issues under discussion here touch on the big questions facing, among others, cultural and religious theory, theoretical physics, and the practical activities of lawmakers. Living in a city where a great many people regard, for example, the problem of restoring animal sacrifice not as narrative material for cultural theorists or nuanced rabbinic interpretation, but as a matter to be taken up by civil engineers, urban planners, and city councilors, the questions of time and historicism, the ontology of Hope, and the convolution of these issues in the immediate applicability of messianic principle demand my attention both as intellectual pursuit and as public policy. As my emails suggest, my thinking on these questions conceives of the future as the direct outcome of the present, not in the "empty" mechanistic sense often attributed to science, and not ignoring thematic or holistic causal relationships, but without minimizing the centrality of our collective responsibility and the real possibility of failure. As stated by Marx, paraphrasing Deuteronomy 30:11–20, it is our actions today that will lead us either to a revolutionary reconstitution of society at large or to common ruin. Thus, my partial answers probably offer little reassurance to one who asks how we may imagine the future as also the product of some superseding principle of optimism.

In the present discussion we have stayed clear of what may be called strong messianism. In some other possible dialog, proceeding without some form of the popular conventions, which for lack of a less pejorative term may be called realism (the possibility of identifying chronological sequence, a set of principles that limit what may be accepted as causality, the relevance of empirical observation, a preference for reductionism and algorithmic explanation), our concern for the future would diminish in urgency. When we succeed in rejecting the notion that events occurring somewhere we call the past are the primary determinants of events that we suppose will occur somewhere we call the future, along with the notion that this determination, however complex and possibly inaccessible to human understanding, resolves itself through constraining causal principles (whether Newtonian action-reaction or the rules of revenge), then we can be entirely unconcerned with possible futures. Freed of materialist blinders, we turn naturally to a strong messianic principle of time, sequencing the events of the world, not chronologically, but thematically, according to plan, and our concern would naturally turn to discovering our place in this plan. However, our sense of urgency grows precisely because we accept the essential historicist core that underlies, but is not identical with, realist thinking. The recent tendency of powerful government figures to connect-the-dots via strong messianism provokes this urgency and does not encourage our admiration for their ability to deconstruct historicist conceptions of time. The problem of time is considered an open question even among physicists who accept an essential historicism (there are few surviving realists among theoretical physicists), but not at the mesoscopic scale appropriate to government policymaking. Perhaps the relevant commentary on the circumstances under which we find this realist answer insufficient is to be found in the writing of Walter Benjamin's friend Gershom Scholem, who had much to say on the relationship between messianic thinking and historical calamity.

If the question of facing the future can only be made sensible under essentially familiar assumptions of time and causality, then we have thrown it back into the realm of history, politics, and law. What role might optimism play in this picture? If there is reason for anticipating a positive future in a materialist worldview, it must rely on a causal principle that constrains the possible ways in which the past can influence the future. Statements of physical law can often be simplified when expressed, in a manner reminiscent of thematic narrative, as goals or constraints, as when the complicated dynamics of objects subject to multiple forces can be summarized by a governing principle which states that the dynamics must follow the course that leads to the minimum final energy configuration. Similarly, special relativity can be summarized in the Principle of Relativity, which states that all observers will measure the same velocity of a light beam, regardless of the observer's point of view. By extension, even while respecting commitment to a simplistic realism, it is not illogical to propose a Principle of Hope, that is, to posit some dynamical principle governing human relationships that functions so as to rule out certain undesirable outcomes. It is not even necessary, logically, to identify the mechanisms for the implementation of the principle. Nevertheless, a question facing us when we propose such a constraint is, "How do we recognize empirical support for our rule, and have we as yet recorded such support?" To posit the Principle of Hope, as was frequently done in the 2004 U.S. presidential election, but support its existence only by repeating our emotional need to believe that it exists, exposes another danger at the Moment of Danger. History reports no shortage of critical moments at which the emotional need for comfortable belief was substituted, at terrible price, for the hard work of doing the right thing. At very least, we must admit that the entirely respectable human need to think comforting thoughts is an inadequate guide to practical conflict resolution, as it encourages each of the conflicting sides to regard their mutually incompatible—even mutually delegitimizing—positions as correct.

While a materialist might consistently adduce evidence for Hope based on claims of human progress (not a universally shared observation), the structural argument is often taken to be more convincing. Whether through the fulfillment of our inner natures (as conceived by Locke, Lévi-Strauss, or Buddha) or the grand whirling of the historical dialectic (as conceived by Hegel, Marx, or Weber), an argument can be built for optimism, at least in regard to the long term. This optimism is not absolute of course—great clashes of good and evil may appear as necessary stages, or as Freud imagined, we may be forced to perpetually walk the razor's edge between the chaos of our destructive natures and the liberation we manage to impose on ourselves by building institutions and respecting our commitment to law (whether lawfulness requires stasis or revolution at any given time). The potency of such willingness to honor the commitments, obligations, and covenants we enter into though inheritance may provide another path to Derrida's "emancipatory promise." That promise may not refer to a commitment made to us—ours to redeem, pass along to our progeny, and take as good reason to see inevitable optimism in the dynamics of future events—but is a commitment we accept upon ourselves and bequeath, through the strength of the relationships we build. Much as we take vicarious pleasure in the vision of our "liberated grandchildren," the only path available to us is to mobilize the strength of our commitment to our "enslaved ancestors" (or their unresolved liberation), apply that strength to our actions in the present moment, and build the relationships that will mobilize our grandchildren in the liberation of their own moment, if for no better reason, than in obligation to us (and our desire for their liberation), as their own "enslaved ancestors." One might consider this construct as a messianism made weaker yet, deprived of guarantees, but at least providing a possible mechanism for facing the future.

\

7

Extinction and Difference

I want to begin by explaining why I have chosen to take on here such a large and seemingly nebulous theme as "Extinction and Difference." You might hear in the title echoes of Derrida's famous title, *Writing and Difference*, and indeed it is quite possible that some such echo lies behind my choice. Yet the title is the germ of my remarks, in fact and not merely in name; yet it is not obvious (at least to me) what pertinence Derrida's classic text might have here.

There are, rather, two reasons that I know why I speak of extinction at a conference on sex, religion, and migration. First, it is the *only* response I have to the invitation to participate with you, no doubt a reflection of my current obsessions. Maybe—I would not go so far as to say "I trust"—by the time I have finished you will not think mine to be quite so idiosyncratic an obsession as it might seem at first. I say again "maybe," doubting neither your sympathy nor your perspicuity, but very much aware of how difficult it is to talk about last things, especially without the prop of a redemptive or apocalyptic narrative of faith.

I have already begun to try to articulate this strange, this seemingly neurotic question of extinction, first by asking *why* it seems so hard to articulate. My first answer was closely tied to the tool with which, for the last quarter century, I have tried to think about the presence of the past: the now-canonic figure of Walter Benjamin's angel, face turned away, not only from an illusion of progress in the future as Benjamin emphasized, but also a fortiori from a contemplation of catastrophes rather future than past. Of course, the general culture is not so much informed by Benjamin's "Theses on the Philosophy of History" as I have been—and, it seems, willy-nilly continue to be. So other answers are needed, to a question that I will now pose again in slightly more expanded form thus: Why, given the evidence in our time of catastrophic social regress combined with a relentless, specieswide assault on the very physical conditions of continued human life on this planet, do we appear so helpless to speak rationally and in a secular mode about the prospects of extinction at our own hands?

My purpose here is not to answer the question, but to relate the prospect of extinction to the themes of the conference. Still, any possibility of my making sense in this speaking situation absolutely requires that we be sensitive to our ingrained resistance to contemplate extinction. It is worth dwelling with that resistance a moment longer, therefore, by quoting (by way of Elliot Wolfson) Alfred North Whitehead's observation that if we "cut away the future . . . the present collapses, emptied of its proper content. Immediate existence requires the insertion of the future in the crannies of the present."[1] If Whitehead is correct, we can say that to speak of "the collapse of the future" is to imply collapse in the present, a situation that obviously makes discourse extremely difficult. It is like holding a conference in a hurricane. You have to shout to be heard at all. There is an urgency here; fantastic or no, I am compelled to express it; it is an urgency beyond the wish to convey that one believes global warming is bad because one is a Democrat, as my friend Michael Hatfield so neatly puts it.

But there is—and I am relieved to be able to say it—another potential use to this intervention, focused as it is in a historical way, none the less so historical because oriented toward the future rather than the past, on the very limits of the possibility of speaking, of speaking together. That is, it may be a way to help us stand or see outside or beyond ourselves and thereby articulate, at least fitfully, the question of what we are doing when we gather to speak about sex, religion, and migration—each of which theme, and all of them together, is as I think you will agree inseparably bound with imaginings of time, beginnings and ends, and of course the possibility of continuity. Really, for all we have talked about the power of the past in the present, we are always working with some imagined future in mind. I repeat Whitehead's dictum: "Immediate existence requires the insertion of the future in the crannies of the present." The future is implicit in our caring enough to come together today.

Otherwise, with whom will we have sex?

Otherwise, with what tongue shall we worship or mock?

Otherwise, where shall we go?

I begin with this last question, the question of migration. Our examinations of contemporary migration, and the continuing echoes of recent ones, are inseparable from the notion of "globalization." (I hear your inward groans at hearing the word once again, and I sigh, too.) It seems to me in fact that some of the communications in advance of this conference have referred to it as the "globalization / migration" conference. One obvious difference between the two terms, however, is that migration has been with us since prehistory, whereas globalization—even if it is just imperialism on the scale of the actual world, not just the known world—seems a novelty rather than a recurrence. Globalization, then, seems to involve some kind of periodization within a grand scheme of historical development, whether it is understood primarily as constituting or taking place within a distinctive phase of the trajectory of capitalism, or constituting a distinctively postmodern mode of migration.[2] If globalization implies a certain period, then the most likely candidate in this forum would probably be that commonly designated by critical theorists as "late capital-ism." I have always mistrusted that formulation somewhat, since it inevitably seems to suggest that capitalism has lasted longer than it should have, that it is somehow an anomalous embarrass-ment in our present. "Late capitalism" also seems to express someone's forlorn wish that it be "last capitalism." Maybe, but even so Marx and Engels's question remains; late capitalism could just as likely (not just as well) mean "last capitalism before barba-rism" as "last capitalism before socialism." With the specter of barbarism, at the technological scale of which our species is now capable, we touch again on the dark shore of extinction.

"Migration" seems to carry a somewhat different charge. Mi-gration—particularly when linked, as it is in this conference, to indicia of human difference such as sex and religion—implies both a contingency and a measure of human agency somehow lacking in "globalization." Perhaps difference implies agency to us because we are so used, in recent decades, to the task of in-creasing the range of audible human speaking positions, that is, to training ourselves and others to be able to hear the truth claims of a broader range of human subjects. I wonder, however, whether we are not accustomed in turn to valorizing "agency" as ultimately a force for good, and accordingly imputing both agency and the authority to speak to *some* differences, those with which we im-plicitly understand ourselves to be in some sort of coalition. If so, then it is worth raising the question of difference and agency with respect to the problem of the "repugnant other," a question I pick up briefly later.

Globalization, by contrast, seems to imply no agency that we would think of as personal, but at best institutional agency—often at the level of a dominant class within a dominant nation-state. This, of course, is one of the reasons why it is sometimes pointed out that "globalization" is really a synonym, or better a euphemism, for the extension of American capital domination, especially in the symbolic realm. It may also be why we so rapidly tire of hearing the term. Are we reluctant to think about globalization anymore? Does it merely depress us, rather than, for example, helping us think about the human situation generally?

That a topic may be depressing does not excuse us from addressing it, we who more than anyone else are paid to think about important matters, even if our deliberations have no effect whatsoever on the situation. And, ugly and loaded as the term globalization may be, surely we are indeed talking about a *phenomenon* whose *effects* are global. From where I am looking, those effects are generally disastrous; the phenomenon I have in mind is not, for example, the spread of market liberalism, à la Thomas Friedman or (once upon a time, in a more naïve age) Francis Fukuyama. Rather, I am thinking primarily of the increased pace of resource exploitation and consumption, directed from multiple centers and tied to flexible exploitation of new sources of cheaper labor, which dictates, among other things, that American capitalism *not* be seen as the sole motor of globalization. I am thinking, for example, of increased petroleum use in Asia, which threatens to make my choice between a Hummer and a Prius of relatively little moment to the global future.[3]

Along with my brother Daniel, I have in the past advocated that we consider the notion of diasporas at least one resource in the search to find better means of balancing collective identities with territory. Diaspora is germane here, alongside migration and globalization, and it is itself a phenomenon that can be conceived as including equal measures of migration and of sex, if we limit (as I will here) "sex" to its deployment and regulation in the perpetuation (or breaching) of the boundaries among human groups. As often as not, of course, diaspora involves a good dose of religion as well. And it might be attractive as a more dynamic concept, implying even more "good agency," than the term *migration*.

Yet I have to query now whether the notion of diaspora as any kind of corrective to the limitations of the nation-state has, even in theory, "time to work" given the pace of destruction of the global biosphere. Part of the problem with the proposal, at least as formulated by Daniel and myself in earlier writings,[4] that diaspora serve as a model for the refinement or modification of the nation-state system is that it has not taken into account the extent to which the latter is already weakened by globalization. Thus, for example, it would be necessary to address more thoroughly whether diaspora politics and community tend to become either more unstable or more viciously exclusionary, as the territorial nations with which they are identified become less self-evident and autonomous collective actors in their own right. Or more autonomous: why assume a telos toward weakened states that may not characterize the entirety of globalization, but only its Western face?

This brings me back to the mundane fact of increased demand for, and consumption of, petroleum in Asia, especially China. The extraction of petrochemicals throughout the world is both a prime instance of the effect of globalization (inasmuch as it places new systemic stresses on the links among politics, production, transportation, and communication), and, as we burn up the world around us, the primary motor of any trajectory toward extinction that may ground in intersubjective reality this specter of extinction that haunts me. It is not only that the pace of extraction of petrochemicals and their simultaneous consumption has increased to the point where one coherent question is whether the resources themselves or our systems based on their exploitation will give out first. In a larger, geohistorical sense, the extraction of petrochemicals is also a kind of "time-space compression" à la David Harvey,[5] an odd replay of the extinctions that produced those fossil fuels in the first place—they are themselves products of death, unless we accept the "abiotic" theory of petroleum.

I daresay Harvey never imagined the application of his "time-space compression" phrase to apply in geological time, to prehistory coming back to bite us like some reincarnated, carnivorous dinosaur. But desperate times call for desperate concepts. In its near-ubiquity (hardly surprising, given its referent), the term *globalization* seems at times aggressively to challenge our capacity for an imaginative discourse adequate in any way to a responsibility for our species and its future.

Note that, as "we" all too commonly do, I keep using the collective nouns "we" and "us." Who are "we" here? The universe of users of the term "globalization?" Is the concept itself global? What does it mean even to speak, as we are wont to do, of "our species" without presuming or reinforcing a perhaps unwanted sameness? Perhaps the human "we" is best identified as the set of those who are aware of their own mortality and who try to compensate for it in some way, an impulse that might explain a lot about both sex and religion. Perhaps not: some of us seem to be able to acknowledge mortality and move on. Thus a television interviewer asked Bob Woodward, commenting on George W. Bush's confidence in his own decision to initiate the current war in Iraq, "Do you know anybody else who's that sure of himself?"

Woodward replied, "I really don't. And Bush's argument is, it was a considered decision. It was necessary. That's his job. Only he had all the information and arguments. And in the end, when you ask him, as I did, 'How's history going to judge this?'—he kind of shrugs. History, we won't know. We'll all be dead."[6] Meaning, presumably, either that we cannot be too distracted by worrying about the future consequences of our deeds and how they will be judged, or more radically, that we cannot know and should not worry whether there will be a future in which something called "history" could be perpetuated—and it does not matter, because "we'll all be dead." That makes "we" the set of those speaking to each other in any given present, which is, after all, perhaps the most pragmatic definition from a linguistic point of view.

Still I offer, once again for your consideration, the notion that globalization implicitly bears with it at least a hint of a foul odor of decay, of extinctions (in the plural) if not necessarily extinction in the absolute. Globalization likewise connotes an anxiety about an inexorable march toward increasing human sameness, a perverted vision of modern ideals of human solidarity. That anxiety has been explicitly acknowledged, for example by Regina Bendix, who asserts in a critique of modern ethnographic and folklore practice, "Behind the assiduous documentation and defense of the authentic lies an unarticulated anxiety of losing the subject."[7] Others, and I think of James Clifford as a respected and prominent example, counter the trope of disappearing uniquenesses (which long predates the notion of globalization) with assertions that the pure products do not fade away, but if anything, "go crazy"—that difference is robust and that, if anything, metropolitan anxiety about the fragility of marginal difference may be an effect of unacknowledged colonial paternalism. Moreover, it may be pointed out, as my friend Martin Land has suggested to me, that sameness is basically an impossible outcome from an evolutionary point of view. Yet, likely or not, this suggests that the *prospect* of sameness is indeed closely linked to the prospect of extinction, since the accession of a stable sameness would mean that evolution had stopped, at least within a circumscribed realm of life on earth. By the same token, an evolutionary perspective implies a contrary positive correlation between diversification and continuity.

My emphasis so far seems to be on cultural developments, as if these took place in a realm distinct from that of what we like to call "power." I certainly do not deny that the anxiety over a prospect of inevitably expanding sameness might also be more pointedly described as a threat of expanding the realm of applicability of certain economic and legal structures, but I am here either assuming that to be the case or bracketing the question of the material base of the changes I am discussing, because I am focusing instead on the imaginative telos that arises in this context. This question of telos is critically relevant, of course, to any consideration of sex and religion. Once again, Whitehead: without a future, even one assumed almost as we assume we will take in oxygen in our next breath, the present can scarcely be imagined. What that means most pertinently here and now is that in a telos of extinction differences of sex, religion, and location, and any possibility of discussing them at a conference or in an edited volume, disappear.

This is, I think, why I have always been extraordinarily moved by David Bowie's song "Five Years," from the album *The Rise and Fall of Ziggy Stardust and the Spiders from Mars*. Bowie presents the scenario: "News had just come over, we had five years left to cry in," positing that the most appropriate or at any rate the most likely collective response to impending extinction is to mourn. Intriguingly, given our own mass resistance to incontrovertible evidence of global degradation, Bowie posits a collective acknowledgment of the news: "so many mothers [were] sighing," and "I knew he was not lying." The news certainly upsets conventional relations of gender and religion: "Cop knelt and kissed the feet of the priest/and the queer threw up at the sight of that." The news of impending extinction inspires a dissociation from self: "I felt like an actor," along with a desire for home and maternity: "I thought of Ma, and I wanted to get back there." "Race" is appealed to as a precious marker of difference during this last long collective human breath. Most broadly, the news inspires a sense of need for the entirety of the species, both collectively *and* in their difference—fat-skinnies, tall-shorts, nobodies, somebodies.

Around the same time, and in a rather different register, Woody Allen did not shrink at expressing the prospect of extinction. He writes: "More than at any time in history, we are at a crossroads. One path leads to despair and utter hopelessness, the other to total extinction. Let us pray that we have the wisdom to choose correctly."[8]

I will not kill this gem with exegesis, except to note that its humor comes from the parody of a rhetoric of fateful choice where in truth there is no saving action possible. But why, in fact, do we equate extinction with despair? Why should we fear extinction? Is it not just part of development? I am not only thinking of biological evolution here. Cultures, collective identities, come and go. Linguists talk about "channels of systematic extinction," as in Marvin Herzog's classic essay on the historical tendency toward normatization in the dialectology of East European Yiddish.[9]

This kind of normatization, necessarily entailing the extinction of older localisms, was linked at least in an earlier period to the formation of national "imagined communities," and you will no doubt recall that something we can now recognize as the formation, the autonomous crystallization of such imagined communities into a global family of nations was once considered a central mark of human progress. Here, in the idea of creation and sustenance of new, stable nation-states that avoided the disruptions of mass migration was one attempt to balance a liberal notion of sustainable difference with a complex notion of unity. As Liisa Malkki cogently argues, however, in the internationalist vision the family resemblance of members of the family of nations was presumed, and almost required, to trump their variety.[10]

Sameness, then, would be a measure of progress. But what is left of that notion, as battered as the very notion of a modernity that is both present and superior to all past moments—and necessarily so?

Having placed so severely into question our ideologies of progress, is it not time also to question the residual category of the "reactionary?" "Reactionary," chauvinist, or tribalist discourses famously employ mechanisms of group boundary maintenance that are intimately related to kinship, that is, to projections of stable group identity forward and backward through time, to and fro in space. One such mechanism is the reiteration of the name, a profoundly human response to "our" awareness of death, a connection pointedly obvious in Ashkenazi Jewish culture where the reiteration of the name is forbidden while its earlier bearer is still alive. It is equally obvious, however, that even traditions of given-again names do not reflect an actual stability or a "myth of the eternal return," for there must have been a first Jewish woman named Shprintse, whose meaning of hope we would more readily recognize in its cognate Esperanza, and she must have been given the name in a Romance language–speaking region rather than some ancient independent Jewish kingdom.

Other mechanisms of group perpetuation are, of course, less innocuous, even repugnant. But can we resist our own impulses and address "even" reactionary identity formations as part of a range of human responses to the implicit link between increasing sameness and the specter of extinction? If we try to do this, and I can only suggest such an exercise now, there are several potential lessons. I can think of two for now. One, suggested to me by Michael Hatfield, is a possible increase in understanding of our own habits of political categorization, by considering as a form of projection onto others as "reactionary" our own, inchoate, unarticulated impulses to turn inward, to retrench and try to deal with the well-being only of those closest to us in the face of an impending systemic collapse that we sense at the edge of our vision but are reluctant quite to acknowledge. Second, we might make some "progress" at understanding ways in which discourses of difference commonly dismissed as reactionary might be occluded attempts at a creative response to the projected telos of sameness and extinction. Imagine, to retroject for a moment, that a tribe of Gentiles listening to Paul's preaching had said: "No thanks, we don't want to be Abraham's heirs, 'even' according to the promise—and if you don't go away and stop preaching to us that we should, we'll kill you!" Sounds reasonable when I put it that way, doesn't it?

Yes, now in order to illuminate our apparent trajectory toward the future, I resort to a projection backward, taking as a touchstone the late antique context in which Paul, anticipating an imminent Messianic redemption "to deliver us from the present evil age" (Galatians 1:3), proleptically announced the end of significant differences among human groups. (Or did he?) Let me be clear that I am not taking sides on controversies regarding the Pauline canon, just reading the Revised Standard Version; hence, there is a limit to how much further evidence I could be deriving from late antiquity for an explanatory link between apocalyptic expectations and views about sameness and difference. Which is not to say that such debates over the real Paul are in any sense *secondary*, since the invocation of figures such as Paul is a resource for rhetorical authority, and hence for collective human action toward extinction or survival, today. As Elliot Wolfson puts it, in a lucid statement of the relation between philology and interpretation, "my telling of time cannot be disentangled from my time of telling."[11]

Paul's universalism is legend, although *pace* Marc Shell,[12] he did not announce an end to kinship—preserving at any rate "rhetorical kinship," that is, a rhetoric of kinship with implications for heritage. Thus, Paul states "there is neither Jew nor Greek . . . [but] you are Abraham's offspring according to the promise" (Galatians 3:28–29). Another citation, from the deutero-Pauline Ephesians (2:14–16) is even more to the point here, because it posits not just an irrelevance of difference but also a process of abolition of difference: "For he is our peace, who has made us both one, and has broken down the dividing wall of hostility, by abolishing in his flesh the law of commandments and ordinances, that he might create in himself one new man in place of the two, so making peace" (Ephesians 2:14–16).

Paul is here speaking to those whom he calls erstwhile "Gentiles," once "strangers to the covenants of promise, having no hope and without God in the world" (Ephesians 2:12). So there is a twofold move demanded here. The Gentiles are brought into some place of promise formerly reserved for an elect sex/religion group, yet only through a loss of specificity, of difference; only "unity" provides "peace." As if to challenge my hypothesis linking *difference* with *survival*, there seems to be an equation here of unity with redemption. Again, not an alien theme for modernity! Nor is the specter of persistent or proliferating differences linked to destruction alien to modernity.

This Paul, so far, sounds like a globalizer. But I have just claimed that globalization is a phenomenon particular to late capitalism. This is indeed projection backward! What do I mean by "projecting backward"? Is that different from retrojection? Is one a logical move, the other merely an unhelpful indulgence in presentism? It is obvious that the present is meaningless without a past that shaped it, but if the present demands a future as well, then it seems there is ultimately little ontological difference between our future and past imaginaries, as Merleau-Ponty suggests: "If it can be said that all prospection is anticipatory retrospection, it can equally well be said that all retrospection is remembered prospection."[13]

If that sounds terribly abstract, let us look at the passage in 1 Corinthians 7:17–31, where Paul states that "every one [should] lead the life which the Lord has assigned to him," following criteria not limited to ethnicity; just as the circumcised should remain such and the uncircumcised remain as they are, so too should the slave never mind his servitude. These worldly things are of naught (my words, not those of the RSV!), "for the appointed time has grown very short" and "the form of this world is passing away."

Meanwhile, the Rabbis devised strategies for stabilizing Jewish identity and difference in the face of deferred redemption. These prominently, and most pertinently here, involved "powers of diaspora" not only for maintaining bonds of kinship (always a function of *language*, of being spoken, as Pierre Legendre has tirelessly reminded us) but also for continually repairing some fiction of continuity of group identity. This might lead us to Jewishness as a potential resource for thinking about strategies both of continuing to articulate difference and of not merely neutralizing, but harnessing, difference in the face of human survival in the present, and in various ways I think that has been my work for the past few decades. There is no lack of prophetic concern for all of humanity, in its difference; there is no lack of Rabbinic awareness of nature, of the contingency of creation; there is a storehouse of evocative phrases, famously including *tikkun olam*, roughly, the maintenance of the world—although traditionally, more along the lines of keeping the pipes from clogging than of rebuilding the foundations, as seems required today.

Why is it, then, that I am not especially enthusiastic at the prospect of marshalling such Jewish tropes as *tikkun olam* in response to that specieswide threat? Perhaps one reason is that they tend to rely on "hope" that the world is not irrevocably broken, and I try very hard not to rely on hope. More particularly and more pertinent here, even their evocations of eternity rarely seem to escape an assumption that the Jewish people—and *a fortiori* at least a portion of the human species—is eternal, as when the Psalmist writes of his confidence that "The counsel of Hashem will endure forever / the designs of His heart throughout the generations" (Psalm 33:11). This is a touchingly human measure of eternity, but obviously one that offers relatively scant guidance once we confront a secular possibility of extinction. If the Psalmist had trouble distinguishing between eternity and the span of human consciousness, how much more so *ani kotonti*, little me, lower-case "i": An earlier attempt of mine to give an account of the at least potentially positive linkage between transgenerational identification and reduced need to accumulate[14] has been criticized, not quite unjustly, as anamnestic sentimentalism. Indeed, my own attachment to the perpetuation of Jewish distinctiveness and "separate" transgenerational memory seems to pale somewhat now, in the face of the broader threats to the species represented by what Arthur Waskow calls "global scorching," the general compulsive consumption of the planet and the inattention to human welfare attendant on the exercise of power by those who differentiate themselves from "the reality-based community."

I pose, accordingly, a less personalized question: How are twentieth-century rationales for anamnestic attachments to particularized identities and politicized memories placed in question by the prospect of extinction? I am thinking, as has been implicit all along, primarily of human extinction (or, short of that, a cataclysmic decline in population), but I do not mean to imply a sharp boundary between that question and other species extinctions, actual or potential. To the contrary, I imagine that as our own lifeworld becomes degraded we are less sensitized to the loss of entire categories of fellow creatures, both more distant and closer relatives. How shocked I was about a year ago when I tried to discuss the mountain gorillas with my teenage son, and he told me, though not thoughtlessly, that there were some things he just couldn't worry about. How sad a moment compared to my pride when, as a kindergartener, he came home and reported that *he* at least, of those in his class, knew that people were animals, too.

Rather discouraging, but if there is anything constructive I am trying to bring out with all these ruminations, it is that while the pair of *difference and identity* cannot be neatly contrasted with that of *redemption and extinction*, a greater "anthropological" (not specialized, but specieswide) capacity to balance the former pair is indispensable if we are ever to imagine (once again!) redemption as more likely than extinction.

Because the secular "we," ecumenical in our ambitions to form a coalition of oppositional or emergent differences into a more responsive and more democratic organization of the species and its lifeworld, are hardly in the ascendant these days, it appears that any change in the telos I am projecting will require, among other intellectual, political, and ethical efforts, an encounter with the *repugnant other.* By that phrase, I intend, pragmatically, any category of other with whom we refuse *as a matter of principle* to empathize because we continue to assume, reflexively, that do so is a betrayal of our own "true selves." Revealingly, that repugnant other would seem to be, in the United States, those not in the purview of this conference because their sexuality and their religion are defined by rootedness rather than migration. "Sex, Religion, and Stable Farm Communities" hardly sounds like the likely title for a conference at Yale. To a remarkable degree, the boundaries of this collective repugnant other's realm remain geographical—recall (it seems ancient history now) not only the map of blue and red states after the elections of 2000 and 2004, but also the graphic suggestion of a reconfiguration of the North American polity into the United States of Canada on one hand, and Jesusland (be still, my typing fingers—not "Jewland") on the other. And geography, fixed place in the old-fashioned sense, remains a stubborn constraint, as for example when we try to speculate in an ethically responsible way about how to act as our lifeworld suffers further degradation. Thus, Michael Hatfield wonders in correspondence with me: "Can we 'go reactionary' on a personal level of buying windmills and planting gardens and giving up our opinions on *New York Times* articles, while at the same time dealing with the Mexicans / whites / blacks / Democrats / Republicans /

evangelicals / Catholics / gays down the road?" And then he instantly points out that even "the one criterion that seems okay in survival mode is those physically around us without regard to differences, but that's the geography-based idea that's at the root of nationalism, isn't it?"

This friend lives in Lubbock, Texas, squarely in Jesusland, and now I myself am from Kansas. That graphic is cute and it may have provided us with a dose of soothing schadenfreude, but it should not let us lapse into reification of these differences. These repugnant others, these domestic reactionaries, are (significantly from an anthropologist's perspective) still not a category of others with whom "we" would refuse to create kinship ties, much as we might rue the prospect of overly right-wing in-laws. Nor is the political divide yet quite coterminous with religious divisions, although it appears increasingly impossible to sustain religious identification across significant political differences—a trend that could indeed lead in turn to sex and marriage prohibitions, that is, to new endogamies. But the point remains that people in your so-called Jesusland are *not all the same*. They are, to start with an obvious and perhaps even a seemingly trivial point, nearly all descendants of immigrants and all bearing histories of migration and loss, heritages that are not necessarily relegated to a forgotten social history, but that can be *engaged* as object lessons in the ways that difference and hybridity are inevitably interwoven. This is done, for example, in Louise Erdrich's recent novel *The Master Butcher's Singing Club*, which is all about ethnicity and memory and mixing and also prominently about "extinctions," of the Native Americans and the Jews, and about the new, contingent differences that come in the midst of and after these extinctions.

What kind of self-interrogation of "we," the collective that might take upon itself this hypothetical encounter with the repugnant other, is required? What questions, for example, about its persistent habit of practicing the discursive "study" of questions such as the links among sex, religion, and migration in various ways *other* than as they affect the possibility of continued human existence and hence, any discourse at all? Does not this form of study amount to a continued practice of enlightenment, aimed at producing greater tolerance? Why do we think this is a helpful endeavor?

The ecologist Wes Jackson, of the Land Institute near Salinas, Kansas, recently shared an essay called "Toward an Ignorance-Based World View."[15] He makes adequately clear that what he has in mind is not know-nothingism but humility toward the complexity of systems that sustain life, and the consequences of massive human interference with them. The essay concludes:

> I've been around a fair number of universities, and I've witnessed friends and the children of friends from creationist homes go to college and graduate, some of them cum laude, and they're still creationists. Cultural and regional history overrode education.
>
> I give this example because here is a question that goes beyond the available answers: Why? If cultural and regional history overrides educational power, what do we do? If education isn't good enough, what do educators do?
>
> Well, maybe it's time to start with a certain amount of humility and say we're fundamentally ignorant about the way minds change. Acknowledging that we are fundamentally ignorant, we now can ask a question that goes beyond the available answers, and that's going to force knowledge out of its categories.

If education, enlightenment, is not the answer, what is to be done? We might perhaps start by questioning the quick assumption that a deterministic cultural and regional history is the only way to explain the apparent, and apparently increasing, ineffectuality of secular education about the contingent nature of human existence and collective human responsibility for the collective human future. Still, it is perhaps a sign of our social limitation, of the ways we are determined by our cultural and regional history, to suppose that there is anything other than education (save political dominance, which we surely do not envision any time soon) that might lead to a situation where another conference, reassessing (for example) the relations among sex, religion, and migration, might be imaginable a full century hence.

Epilogue

On my bookshelf, as yet unopened, lies a volume by James Howard Kunstler, *The Long Emergency: Surviving the End of Oil, Climate
Change, and Other Converging Catastrophes of the Twenty-First Century*. On my list of books to read, not yet ordered, is Giorgio
Agamben's *State of Exception*. I know without seeing Agamben's
book that his title is an allusion to Walter Benjamin's famous saying, in reference to the suspension of civil rights, that "the 'state
of emergency' in which we live is not the exception but the rule."[1]
    Kunstler's and Agamben's titles point respectively to our spe-
cies' critical failures to maintain its own lifeworld and to integrate
adequately the personhood of each human organism with the
commonality of every *Homo sapiens* past, present, and future.
Both of those kinds of failings loom in tandem ever larger. Walls
are built between humans in the Southwest, between Israel and
Palestine, between neighborhood and neighborhood in Baghdad.
Wealthy collectives contemplate seawalls to contain the literal
floodwaters to come, while levees of nationalist rhetoric are desperately thrown up in an attempt to turn away refugees from portions of the planet whose people have been "globalized" into
destitution.
    All this may do nothing more than signal my right thinking,
and merely mentioning these crises does nothing toward their
resolution. The reflections in this book are, inevitably, humanly

inadequate—inadequate in a characteristically human way, and inadequate to the current needs of the species. There are, as best I can determine, two reasons why they may be useful nevertheless. One is that a particular group identity—Jewishness—that has been a vital voice and a critical trope for discussions of humanity and difference in the "West" remains, along with other group identities, both a resource and a diagnostic site in our efforts to respond to the "long emergency" we are already facing. The second is that extension in timespace is not merely an "objective" way of describing humans, individually, at the level of the group or the species as a whole; it is also critical to the rhetorics of identity with which, in turn, we forge our projects toward death, our projects of keeping on.

Introduction

1. John Dewey, *Art as Experience* (New York: Milton, Balch and Company, 1934), 23.

2. Gayle Rubin, "The Traffic in Women," in Rayna R. Reiter, ed., *Toward an Anthropology of Women* (New York: Monthly Review Press, 1975), 157–210.

3. Hannah Arendt, *The Human Condition* (Garden City, N.Y.: Anchor Books, 1958), 153–154.

4. These two senses of "culture" might map usefully, if imperfectly, onto the distinction between "cultural anthropology" and "philosophical anthropology."

5. Dewey, *Art as Experience*, 13.

6. Andreas Gotzmann and Christian Wiese, eds., *Modern Judaism and Historical Consciousness: Identities, Encounters, Perspectives* (Leiden: Brill, 2007), 475–493. I am grateful for permission to reprint.

7. First published in *Cardozo Law Review* 26:3 (2005), 119–138.

Chapter 1

1. Jacques Derrida, "Racism's Last Word," *Critical Inquiry* 12 (1985): 290–299.

2. I know: the "correct" citation is to Denise Riley, *Am I That Name?* (Minneapolis: University of Minnesota Press, 1989).

3. Derrida, "Racism's Last Word," 292.

4. George Lakoff and Mark Johnson, *Philosophy in the Flesh: The Embodied Mind and Its Challenge to Western Thought* (New York: Basic Books, 1999), 95.

5. Gayatri Chakravorti Spivak, "Can the Subaltern Speak?" in Cary Nelson and Lawrence Grossberg, eds., *Marxism and the Interpretation of Culture* (Urbana: University of Illinois Press, 1988), 271–313.

6. I pause in this list to suggest an instructive contrast between Walter Benjamin's "strong" version of identification with the ancestors (as he wrote, "even the dead will not be safe from the enemy if he wins") and our own

contemporary David Biale's marvelous attempt, in the edited volume *Cultures of the Jews: A New History* (New York: Schocken Books, 2002), at making them less strange. Of course, Biale's book is not structured according to ancestry, but rather in line with a model of cultural translation that makes, for example, Alexandrine Jews in the third century or Ferraran Jews in the sixteenth our contemporaries.

7. George Lakoff and Mark Johnson, *Metaphors We Live By* (Chicago: University of Chicago Press, 1980), 4.

8. Latkes are vegetable pancakes—here, clearly referring to the potato pancakes that are a traditional Ashkenazi Jewish food for the holiday of Hanukkah. Hamantashen are the traditional Ashkenazi pastry for the holiday of Purim. Years ago, the subject of which was to be preferred, on any grounds whatsoever, became the subject of annual mock debates staged each year at the University of Chicago, in which academics from various disciplines have deployed the rhetorics of their special fields to brilliant parodic effect. The tradition continues and has, I believe, spread. See Ruth Fredman Cernea, ed., *The Great Latke-Hamantash Debate* (Chicago: University of Chicago Press, 2006).

9. Edmond Jabès, *Le Livre de l'hospitalité* (Paris: Gallimard, 1991), 55.

10. Howard Eilberg-Schwartz, *The Savage in Judaism: An Anthropology of Israelite Religion and Ancient Judaism* (Bloomington: Indiana University Press, 1990).

11. Daniel Boyarin, *Carnal Israel: Reading Sex in Talmudic Culture* (Berkeley: University of California Press, 1993).

12. Miriam Bodian, *Hebrews of the Portuguese Nation: Conversos and Community in Early Modern Amsterdam* (Bloomington: Indiana University Press, 1997).

13. Eric Hobsbawm and Terence Ranger, eds., *The Invention of Tradition* (Cambridge: Cambridge University Press, 1983).

14. Benedict Anderson, *Imagined Communities: Reflections on the Origin and Spread of Nationalism* (London: Verso, 1983).

15. Brigitte Miriam Bedos-Rezak, "The Confrontation of Orality and Textuality: Jewish and Christian Literacy in Eleventh- and Twelfth-Century Northern France," in Gabrielle Sed-Rajna, ed., *Rashi, 1040–1990: Hommage à Ephraim E. Urbach* (Paris: Editions Cerf, 1993), 551.

Chapter 2

1. This remains a confused question, partly because anthropologists sometimes remain defensively possessive about "their" culture concept, while scholars writing from training or housing in literature departments sometimes seem casually voyeuristic as they dip into analyses of daily culture outside the academy. In any case, it was within the Modern Language

Association, sometime in the early 1990s, that I was able to help establish a Discussion Group on Jewish Cultural Studies.

2. Herbert Gutman is the author of *Work, Culture and Society in Industrializing America* (London: Blackwell, 1977) and *The Black Family in Slavery and Freedom, 1750–1925* (New York: Pantheon Books, 1976), among other works.

3. See Johannes Fabian, *Time and the Other: How Anthropology Makes Its Object* (New York: Columbia University Press, 1983).

4. See Harvey Goldberg, "Coming of Age in Jewish Studies, Or Anthropology Is Counted in the Minyan," *Jewish Social Studies* 4, no. 3 (1998): 29–64.

5. See also Eric R. Wolf, *Europe and the People Without History* (Berkeley: University of California Press, 1982).

6. Daniel Boyarin and Jonathan Boyarin, eds., *Jews and Other Differences: The New Jewish Cultural Studies* (Minneapolis: University of Minnesota Press, 1996), vii.

7. In truth, I had never had a home in the academy before 2004.

8. "He has had a taste of Paradise."

9. Clifford Geertz, "Thick Description: Toward an Interpretative Theory of Culture," in *The Interpretation of Cultures* (New York: Basic Books, 1973).

10. I am extremely grateful to the members of the History Department (as of the Religious Studies Department) at the University of Kansas for welcoming me as the first Robert M. Beren Professor of Modern Jewish Studies there, as I am to Jeremy Zwelling at Wesleyan University for inviting me to teach a Jewish history course in the fall of 2004, even if those generous acts may slightly undermine my argument in this essay.

11. JC did not add "no pun intended," indicating, to my mind, that no pun was in fact intended.

12. *The Jew and the Other* (Ithaca, N.Y.: Cornell University Press, 2004), x.

13. Judith M. Lieu, *Christian Identity in the Jewish and Graeco-Roman World* (Oxford: Oxford University Press, 2004), 302.

14. Maria Rosa Menocal, *The Arabic Role in Medieval Literary History: A Forgotten Heritage* (Philadelphia: University of Pennsylvania Press, 1987), cited in Ammiel Alcalay, *After Jews and Arabs: Remaking Levantine Culture* (Minneapolis: University of Minnesota Press, 1993), 23.

15. Roberto Bonfil, *Jewish Life in Renaissance Italy* (Berkeley: University of California Press, 1994), 1.

16. Ibid., xi.

17. Robert Chazan, *Fashioning Jewish Identity in Medieval Western Christendom* (Cambridge: Cambridge University Press, 2004), ix.

18. These examples are drawn from works I have read and taught with great profit, and I hope that my *Randbemerkungen* will not be taken as carping.

19. Miriam Bodian, *Hebrews of the Portuguese Nation: Conversos and Community in Early Modern Amsterdam* (Bloomington: University of Indiana Press, 1997), 102.

20. "Families and Their Fortunes," in David Biale, ed., *Cultures of the Jews: A New History* (Berkeley: University of California Press, 2002), 573–636, at 617.

21. Bonfil, *Jewish Life in Renaissance Italy*, 1.

22. Aron Rodrigue, "The Ottoman Diaspora," in Biale, *Cultures of the Jews*, 863–885, at 879.

23. Yosef Kaplan, "Bom Judesmo: The Western Sephardic Diaspora," in ibid., 639–669, at 646.

24. See H. Aram Veeser, ed., *The New Historicism* (New York: Columbia University Press, 1989).

25. In a lecture given at Wesleyan University on December 2, 2004.

26. See Daniel's *Carnal Israel* (Berkeley: University of California Press, 1993).

27. Daniel Boyarin, *Border Lines: The Partition of Judeo-Christianity* (Philadelphia: University of Pennsylvania Press, 2004).

28. "The Reality of Yiddish Versus the Ghetto Myth: The Sociolinguistic Roots of Yiddish," in *To Honor Roman Jakobson: Essays on the Occasion of His Seventieth Birthday* (The Hague: Mouton, 1967), 3:2,199–2,211, at 2,205.

29. Jeremy Cohen, *Sanctifying the Name of God: Jewish Martyrs and Jewish Memories of the First Crusade* (Philadelphia: University of Pennsylvania Press, 2004).

30. David Nirenberg, "Mass Conversion and Genealogical Mentalities: Jews and Christians in Fifteenth-Century Spain," *Past and Present* 174 (February 2002), 3–41, at 7.

31. Ibid., 39–40.

32. *The Black Atlantic* (Cambridge, Mass.: Harvard University Press, 1993), 81.

Chapter 3

1. Cited in Claude Lefort, *Essais sure le politique* (Paris: Editions Seuil, 1986), 303.

2. A better translation of Marx's phrase might be "the isolation of rural life." See "Notes from the Editor," *Monthly Review*, October 2003.

3. Loren Eiseley, *The Invisible Pyramid* (New York: Charles Scribner's Sons, 1970), 7–8.

4. Stanley Diamond, *In Search of the Primitive: A Critique of Civilization* (New Brunswick, N.J.: Transaction Books, 1974), 197–198.

5. Ibid., 165.

6. Michael Fischer, "Ethnography and the Postmodern Arts of Memory," in James Clifford and George E. Marcus, eds., *Writing Culture: The Poetics and Politics of Ethnography* (Berkeley: University of California Press, 1986), 194–234, at 203. Quoted here by kind permission of Diana Der-Hovanessian.

7. Abraham Joshua Heschel, *Kotsk: In gerangl far emesdikeyt* (Tel Aviv: ha-Menorah, 1973), 1:82 (translation mine).

8. Pierre Legendre, "Prologue," in Alexandra Papageorgiou-Legendre, *Filiation: Fondement généalogique de la psychanalyse* (Paris: Fayard, 1990), 15.

Chapter 4

1. Jack Kugelmass, "Bloody Memories: Encountering the Past in Contemporary Poland," *Cultural Anthropology* 10, no. 3 (1991): 279–301.

2. Adam Phillips, *Darwin's Worms: On Life Stories and Death Stories* (New York: Basic Books, 2000), 120.

3. Ibid., 122.

4. Wallace Markfield, *Teitlebaum's Window* (New York: Knopf, 1970), 150.

5. Ibid., 298.

6. Sherwin Nuland, *Lost in America: A Journey with My Father* (New York: Knopf, 2003), 138–139.

7. Phillip Bobbitt, "Our Approval Ratings Are Way Down," *New York Times*, April 4, 2004.

8. Quoted in Christopher Dickey, "The Story of O," ibid.

Chapter 5

1. www.decoupageforthesoul.com/aboutus.htm.

2. www.iht.com/articles/2002/05/17/edold_ed3_40.php, accessed 5/1/2007.

3. Alfred Kazin, *A Walker in the City* (New York: Harcourt Brace Jovanovich, 1975), 99. See the discussion of Kazin in Julian Levinson, *Exiles on Main Street: Jewish American Writers and American Literary Culture* (Bloomington: Indiana University Press, 2008).

4. John Bush Jones, *Our Musicals, Ourselves* (Waltham, Mass.: Brandeis University Press, 2003), 191.

5. William Least Heat-Moon, *PrairyErth: A Deep Map* (Boston: Houghton Mifflin, 1991), 292.

6. Ibid., 6.

7. Ibid., 7.

8. Marilyn Robinson, *Gilead* (New York: Farrar, Straus & Giroux, 2004), 76.

9. www.ajhs.org/publications/chapters/chapter.cfm?documentID = 196.

10. Salman Rushdie, *The Wizard of Oz* (London: British Film Institute, 1992), 14.

11. Ibid.

12. Ibid., 17.

13. Ibid., 20.

14. Robert Cover, "Nomos and Narrative," in *Narrative, Violence and the Law: The Essays of Robert Cover* (Ann Arbor: University of Michigan Press, 1993), 45.

15. Michael Eigen, *The Sensitive Self* (Middletown, Conn.: Wesleyan University Press, 2003), 5.

16. Rushdie, *The Wizard of Oz*, 60.

Chapter 6

1. Owen Ware, "Dialectic of the Past / Disjuncture of the Future: Derrida and Benjamin on the Concept of Messianism," *Journal for Cultural and Religious Theory* 5 (2004): 99.

2. Jacques Derrida, *Specters of Marx: The State of the Debt, The Work of Mourning, and the New International*, trans. Peggy Kamuf (New York: Routledge, 1994).

3. Ibid., 70.

4. Brian Massumi, "Introduction to Fear: The Politics of Fear: It's Everywhere You Want to Be," www.anu.cdu.au/HRC/first_and_last/works/fear everywhere.htm.

5. Abraham Joshua Heschel, *Kotsk: In gerangl far emesdikeyt* (Tel Aviv: ha-Menorah, 1973), 192.

6. Derrida, *Specters of Marx*, 17.

7. Massumi, "Introduction to Fear."

8. Bruce Ackerman, *Social Justice in the Liberal State* (New Haven: Yale University Press, 1980), 139.

9. See Holly Doremus, "Constitutive Law and Environmental Policy," *Stanford Environmental Law Journal* 22 (2003): 295.

10. Walter Benjamin, "Theses on the Philosophy of History," in *Illuminations* (New York: Schocken Books, 1969), 264.

11. Judith Butler, *Gender Trouble: Feminism and the Subversion of Identity* (New York: Routledge, 1990).

12. Erin Carlston, *Thinking Fascism: Sapphic Modernism and Fascist Modernity* (Stanford, Calif.: Stanford University Press, 1998), 184.

13. Owen Ware, "Dialectic," 105.

14. Benjamin, "Theses," 264.

15. Hannah Arendt, "Introduction: Walter Benjamin, 1892–1940," in Benjamin, *Illuminations*, 18.

16. Ware, "Dialectic," 107.

17. Ibid., 103.

18. "Social Democracy thought fit to assign to the working class the role of the redeemer of future generations, in this way cutting the sinews of its greatest strength. This training made the working class forget both its hatred and it spirit of sacrifice, for both are nourished by the image of enslaved ancestors rather than that of liberated grandchildren." Benjamin, "Theses," 260.

19. Ware, "Dialectic," 113.

20. Ibid., 104.

21. Ibid., 113.

22. Scholem, "Toward an Understanding of the Messianic Idea in Judaism," in *The Messianic Idea in Judaism and Other Essays on Jewish Spirituality* (New York: Schocken Books, 1971), 3. Scholem's essay was first published in 1959. What is most relevant here, of course, is not the "actual" historical character of traditional Jewish messianism but Benjamin's notion of it, fundamentally shaped by his friendship with Scholem.

23. Ibid., 26 ("For precisely to the extent that the rationalism of the Jewish and European Enlightenment subjected the Messianic idea to an ever advancing secularization, it freed itself of the restorative element").

24. Ibid., 11.

25. Ware, "Dialectic," 100.

26. Derrida, *Specters of Marx*, 99.

27. Eric Hobsbawm, *Age of Extremes: A History of the World, 1914–1991* (New York: Pantheon Books, 1994).

28. Benjamin, "Theses," 264.

29. Ware, "Dialectic," 112.

30. Ibid., quoting Derrida, *Who's Afraid of Philosophy? Right to Philosophy*, trans. Jan Plug (Stanford, Calif.: Stanford University, Press, 2002), 22.

31. Derrida, *Specters of Marx*, 73.

32. Compare this assertion of Edmond Jabès: "Sometimes we have to wait for years before the moment which marked us finds its voice." *The Book of Questions*, trans. Rosemarie Waldrop (Middletown, Conn.: Wesleyan University Press, 1977), 2:29.

33. Robert Chazan, *Jewish Suffering: The Interplay of Medieval Christian and Jewish Perspectives* (Kalamazoo: Medieval Institute Publications, Western Michigan University, 1998), 27.

34. Derrida, *Specters of Marx*, 75.

35. Ibid., 14–15.

36. Ibid., 167.

37. Ibid., 168–169.

Chapter 7

1. Quoted in Elliot Wolfson, *Language, Eros, Being: Kabbalistic Hermeneutics and Poetic Imagination* (New York: Fordham University Press, 2005), xviii.

2. See Amitav Ghosh, "The Diaspora in Indian Culture," *Public Culture* 2, no. 11 (1989): 423.

3. Jab Mouawad and Matthew L. Wald, "The Oil Uproar That Isn't: Prices Cause Concern, but Little Change in Behavior or Laws," *New York Times*, July 12, 2005.

4. Jonathan Boyarin and Daniel Boyarin, *Powers of Diaspora* (Minneapolis: University of Minnesota Press, 2002).

5. David Harvey, *The Condition of Postmodernity: An Enquiry Into the Origins of Cultural Change* (New York: Blackwell, 1989).

6. www.pbs.org/wgbh/pages/frontline/shows/choice2004/bush/core.html.

7. Regina Bendix, *In Search of Authenticity: The Formation of Folklore Studies* (Madison: University of Wisconsin Press, 1997), 3, quoted in Vincent Cheng, *Inauthentic: The Anxiety Over Culture and Identity* (New Brunswick, N.J.: Rutgers University Press, 2004), 32.

8. Quoted in Robert Byrne, *The 637 Best Things Anybody Ever Said* (New York: Athenaeum, 1982), 79.

9. Marvin Herzog, "Channels of Systematic Extinction in Yiddish Dialects," in *For Max Weinreich on His Seventieth Birthday* (The Hague: Mouton, 1964), 93–107.

10. Liisa Malkki, "Citizens of Humanity: Internationalism and the Imagined Community of Nations," *Diaspora* 3, no. 1 (1994): 41–68.

11. Wolfson, *Language, Eros, Being*, xvi.

12. Marc Shell, *The End of Kinship: "Measure for Measure," Incest, and the Idea of Universal Siblinghood* (Stanford, Calif.: Stanford University Press, 1988).

13. Merleau-Ponty, *The Phenomenology of Perception*, 414, cited by Wolfson, *Language, Eros, Being*, at xxviii. Would Martin Land agree? See Chapter 6.

14. See Chapter 3.

15. Wes Jackson, "Toward an Ignorance-Based World View," *The Land Report* 81 (Spring 2005): 14–16.

Epilogue

1. Walter Benjamin, *Illuminations* (New York: Schocken Books, 1969), 257.